Just Warriors, Inc.

The Ethics of Privatized Force

Deane-Peter Baker

continuum

Continuum International Publishing Group
The Tower Building   80 Maiden Lane
11 York Road   Suite 704
London SE1 7NX   New York NY 10038

www.continuumbooks.com

British Library Cataloguing-in-Publication Data
A catalogue record for this book is available from the British Library.

ISBN: HB: 978-1-4411-1172-2
         PB: 978-1-4411-3417-2

Library of Congress Catalog-ing-in-Publication Data
Baker, Deane-Peter.
   Just warriors, Inc. : the ethics of privatized force / Deane-Peter Baker.
      p. cm.
   Includes bibliographical references.
   ISBN 978-1-4411-3417-2 -- ISBN 978-1-4411-1172-2 (pbk.) 1. Private military companies-
-Moral and ethical aspects. 2. Private security services--Moral and ethical aspects.
3. Mercenary troops--Moral and ethical aspects. 4. Defense contracts--Moral and ethical
aspects. 5. Contracting out--Moral and ethical aspects. 6. Privatization--Moral and ethical
aspects. I. Title. II. Title: Just warriors, Incorporated.

   U240.B24 2010
   172'.42--dc22

                                                                    2010005690

Typeset by Servis Filmsetting Ltd, Stockport, Cheshire
Printed and bound in India by Replika Press Pvt Ltd

Contents

Preface

As a young undergraduate I dated a nursing student whose
brother, a former South African Defence Force (SADF) Special
Forces soldier or 'Recce' operator, was at the time working for
what was then a relatively unknown private military company
called Executive Outcomes. Because he was away on contract
in Angola at the time, I only met my then girlfriend's brother on
one occasion (when we joined him for a memorable night on the
town), but I remember being very impressed by his quiet tough-
ness and intrigued at the notion of a private company providing
robust armed forces in support of governments facing rebels and
insurgents. My interest was relatively short-lived, however, and I
soon moved on to other topics (and other girlfriends). Largely by
accident I ended up on a career path as an academic philosopher,
specializing in the epistemology and philosophy of religion, and
for close to a decade the world of Executive Outcomes seemed
to me only of relevance as a mildly amusing anecdote about my
misspent youth.

Then two things happened which changed all that. First, I
met Peter Goldie (now of the University of Manchester) who
pointed out that armed conflict is a perfectly legitimate area
of philosophical enquiry (Peter, in turn, introduced me to his
former Oxford classmate and Rhodes Scholar, David Rodin, a
philosopher of war *par excellence* from whom I have learned an
inestimable amount). Second, I turned on the evening news one
night to see images of my ex-girlfriend's brother and a group

of other former SADF soldiers (plus Simon Mann, formerly of Britain's SAS) under arrest in Zimbabwe on charges related to an alleged attempted coup in Equatorial Guinea. It was only then that I belatedly realized there are a wide range of significant and philosophically interesting questions which arise as a consequence of the private provision of armed force. What, I asked myself, is the difference between what my ex's brother had been doing as an Executive Outcomes contractor while working in the service of the government of Angola, on the one hand, and his reported involvement in the alleged coup plot, on the other? What is it, exactly, that accounts for the negative light in which 'mercenaries' are generally held?

It was these questions and others like them, which led me to organize a conference on the topic 'Private Military Companies, States and Global Civil Society: Ethics, Theory, and Practice'. Held at the Cathedral Peak Hotel, nestled among South Africa's spectacular Drakensberg mountains, it was a memorable affair. It was there that I met many of the people who would go on, in one way or another, to be of enormous help in the process of shaping my thinking on the subject of this book. Among them, Mervyn Frost, Nancy Sherman, Doug Brooks, Asa Kasher and Jessica Wolfendale, are especially deserving of my thanks, as are Andrew Alexandra and Marina Caparini who were my co-editors on the book project that grew out of the conference.

Others I have had the opportunity to engage with along the way, and who have influenced my thought process for this book, include Peter Feaver, Adam Cobb, Steve Biddle and Dominick Donald. The time I spent as a Visiting Research Fellow at the Triangle Institute for Security Studies, which Peter Feaver made possible, was of great value in laying some of the foundations for this project. It was my former colleague at the University of KwaZulu-Natal, Lawrence Piper, who convinced me that writing this book might be a good idea. Lawrence also offered significant insights which have shaped the final product.

I had the opportunity to try out some of the arguments

contained in this book at the excellent Second International Military Ethics Conference in December 2008, which was organized by David Whetham and held at the UK Joint Services Command and Staff College. My thanks must go to the British Academy, which provided David with the grant that made my involvement in the conference possible. I am most grateful for comments received on that occasion. George Lucas in particular was especially insightful and helpful (as is his wont), and inputs by Jessica Wolfendale and Asa Kasher were once again influential. The three months I spent as a Visiting Research Fellow at the US Army War College's Strategic Studies Institute (which would never have happened but for Steve Metz's generous efforts) gave me invaluable writing time. My thanks must also go to the University of KwaZulu-Natal for financial support and for allowing me that period of sabbatical, and to my colleagues in the School of Philosophy and Ethics who carried my workload while I was away.

I've also subjected numerous students – both my own and some from other institutions – to my ruminations on this topic over the past few years. Most endured their guinea-pig status patiently, and some poked helpful holes in early versions of my arguments. My thanks to you all. Conway Waddington, Meghan Spilka O'Keefe, David Pfotenhauer and Michael Pitchford deserve special mention for their intelligent and thoughtful observations. Sadly, publication deadlines for this volume meant I never had the opportunity to bounce the ideas contained herein off the midshipmen I now have the privilege of teaching, nor my current colleagues (both military and civilian) at the US Naval Academy.

The final version of this book would have been considerably poorer were it not for philosophers James Pattison and Ian Jennings, and industry experts Eeben Barlow, Christopher Beese and Doug Brooks, all of whom took time out of extremely busy lives to offer their very valuable thoughts on the book as it took shape. In a more indirect, but no less critical way, my wife Polly selflessly supported and encouraged me throughout. The final vote of thanks must go to my father, Peter Baker, who was painstakingly thorough in checking both my arguments and my grammar. As with all of those I have the privilege of thanking here, we didn't agree on everything, and responsibility for the final product (particularly its faults) lies solely with me.

Parts of this book build on arguments that I have made in previously published papers, and I am grateful for permission to reuse some of that material here. Chapter 2 is largely a revised version of my chapter entitled 'Of "Mercenaries" and Prostitutes: Can Private Warriors be Ethical?' which appeared in Alexandra, Baker and Caparini (eds), *Private Military Companies: Ethics, Policies and Civil-Military Relations* (London: Routledge 2008, pp. 30–42). A summarized version of the argument I made in 'Defending the Common Life: National Defence after Rodin' (*Journal of Applied Philosophy*, 2006, 23(3), pp. 259–75) appears in Chapter 4, and my 'Agency Theory: A New Model of Civil-Military Relations for Africa?' (*African Journal on Conflict Resolution*, 2007, 7(1), pp. 113–36) provided the kernel of my account of Peter Feaver's Agency Theory which runs through chapters 5, 6 and 7.

Introduction

'The use of contractors on the battlefield is no longer an optional or marginal activity.'[1] So writes Mark Cancian, retired US Marine Corps Colonel and respected military analyst. Contractors are a de facto permanent part of the US military's force structure, and should be treated accordingly, Cancian contends. Few analysts with any meaningful grasp of military affairs would be likely to contest this claim. The simple fact is that in the post-Cold War era of reduced defence budgets, few if any countries of the world are able to conduct and sustain major military deployments without contractor support.

While the use of contractors in support of military operations has a long history, their large-scale employment by the US (and to a lesser extent Britain and a handful of other Western nations) in Iraq and Afghanistan in recent years has resulted in considerable controversy. Terms like 'mercenaries', 'war profiteers', 'merchants of death' and 'dogs of war' have been much used in the media. Displaying a flair for the dramatic, Brookings Institute analyst Peter W. Singer has accused the US of replacing the internationally respected 1991 Gulf War 'coalition of the willing' with a 'coalition of the billing' in the more recent conflict in Iraq.[2]

Protests over the employment of contractors have been fuelled by hysteria over the large numbers which have been bandied about. These have varied wildly, but Mark Cancian seems correct in saying that his figure of 265,000 contractor personnel active in Iraq and Afghanistan in the second quarter of the fiscal year

2008 represents a 'fairly reliable' count. The trouble, as Cancian points out, is that there is considerable misunderstanding of what this figure means. There is a widespread misperception that 'the majority of these 265,000 contractors are gun-toting Americans. In fact, few are armed, and 55 percent are Iraqis.'[3] Cancian estimates that only between 6,000 and 7,000 of these contractors actually carry firearms in carrying out their duties. Even that figure does not tell the whole story:

> About three-fourths of these security contractors protect fixed facilities inside major bases and never venture outside the wire. Although the requirement for interior guards was always recognized, a 2005 suicide bombing at a dining facility in Mosul highlighted the need for screening personnel entering heavily populated facilities. Some of these internal security personnel are military, but the majority are contractors. These security guards are generally TCNs [third country nationals]; for example, Salvadorans guard the US Agency for International Development compound in the Green Zone, Ugandans guard facilities for the Marine Corps. The main function of these security guards consists of screening personnel entering facilities by checking identity cards. The majority of this group has never fired a shot in anger. They are more akin to the security guards one sees in the United States guarding banks or shopping malls.[4]

It is the approximately one per cent of contractors who provide bodyguard or 'close protection' services in Iraq and Afghanistan who have captured the headlines and tickled the public's sense of outrage. One company in particular, Blackwater USA,[5] has attracted the lion's share of attention, including being the focus of a sensationalist bestseller written by Jeremy Scahill entitled *Blackwater: The Rise of the World's Most Powerful Mercenary Army*.[6] The book's popularity rests in part on its careful exaggerations about Blackwater's manpower and capabilities, and on claims of politico-religious conspiracy that rival those in Dan Brown's novel *The Da Vinci Code*. Nonetheless there can be little question that Blackwater's actions in Iraq have been noteworthy. Blackwater leaped to international prominence on 30 March 2004 when four of the company's contractors were ambushed and killed in the insurgent hotbed of Fallujah. Their bodies were dragged through the city, mutilated, burned and hung from a bridge – all before the watching eyes of the international media. The incident drew immediate comparisons with the so-called 'battle of Mogadishu' or 'Black Hawk Down incident',[7] which took place in Mogadishu, Somalia in 1993, in which 18 US soldiers were killed, some of their bodies having been similarly mutilated. The incident was also a significant factor leading to the US military's aborted and controversial attempt to 'recapture' Fallujah from insurgents in April 2004. Blackwater again came to prominence when one of the company's protective security details (PSDs) killed 17 Iraqis, allegedly unarmed civilians, in Baghdad's Nisoor Square on 16 September 2007.[8] This incident led to the 2009 Iraqi government decision to deny Blackwater a licence to continue to operate in Iraq, which in turn seems to have led to the company changing its name to Xe and shifting its prime focus from providing armed security contractors to training military and law enforcement personnel at its vast US training facilities.

In general, Cancian's analysis leads him to conclude that, 'there is little to be gained in terms of capability, control, or cost by replacing contractors with military personnel'.[9] He contends that portrayals of the tiny percentage of contractors who provide bodyguard services as 'rogue mercenaries' is largely false, and that these contractors are for the most part 'highly professional'.[10] But, because of the controversial public profile of companies like Blackwater, and related issues, Cancian nonetheless views replacing contracted bodyguards with government personnel as an option 'worth considering', though notes that this 'would not save money'.[11] That is certainly one possibility to be considered, and is arguably the most politically palatable option. But if we step out from under the burden of fickle public opinion for a moment, perhaps we might quietly ask the question whether this is really the best option?

In March 2006 a report alleged that, at an international conference in Amman, Jordan, Cofer Black, then Vice Chairman of
Blackwater USA and former senior anti-terrorism official at the
CIA and US State Department, suggested that Blackwater could
provide a 'a small, nimble, brigade-size force'[12] for rapid deployment to trouble spots around the world. Blackwater later denied
that any such claim had been made, but whatever the truth of
the matter, this is a provocative and interesting idea. It's also not
without precedent. In the 1990s a South African-based company,
Executive Outcomes, provided a small but robust military force
which, in addition to training and advisory services, conducted
direct combat operations on behalf of the Angolan government against União Nacional para a Independência Total de
Angola (UNITA) rebels, and then on behalf of the Sierra Leone
government against the murderous Revolutionary United Front
(RUF).[13] Most commentators agree that Executive Outcomes were
militarily effective, though there was and continues to be much
controversy surrounding the company. In the end the company's close association with South Africa's Apartheid-era security forces made them politically unpalatable, and the company
was disbanded in the late 1990s.

Both Cofer Black's (alleged) comments and Executive Outcomes' actual deployments have been the cause of a great deal
of alarm in the media and civil society organizations. But there
is also a small but increasingly vocal lobby which argues that
the employment of what we might call 'contracted combatants'
is simply a facet of a global trend, namely the move towards
outsourcing what were traditionally government functions. For
example, Mervyn Frost, Professor of International Relations and
Head of the War Studies Department at King's College London,
argues that the private provision of military services

> . . . does not offend or contradict the ethical values built into the most
> fundamental global institutions of our time, global civil society, and,
> the society of democratic states. We who hold civilian and citizenship

rights are entitled to use our rights to create private companies
offering services to other rights holders, provided that in doing so,
we do not abuse the rights of our fellow rights holders. . . . citizens
in democracies might, with good reason, seek to privatize some
functions normally carried out by public bodies. Furthermore . . .
doing this need not offend our fundamental ethical commitments.
Privatization is a public act, by a public authority, for the achievement
of a public good. It involves the creation of an anarchical institution,
for the achievement of public goods. The key . . . is regulation by
public bodies.[14]

Indeed, there is a significant body of academic work emerging
which suggests that the traditional distinctions between public
and private can no longer be unreflectively held to apply. As
Dr Patricia Owens of the Department of Politics at Queen Mary,
University of London writes:

Historically and conceptually, the distinction between the domestic
and the foreign, and between the public and the private, have been
crucial to how we have understood the functioning of modern government and the mobilization of resources to fight in 'national' armies.
. . . The idea that security and insecurity are now experienced and
practiced in ways that merge the internal and external, the public and
private, is an important feature of recent literature on the changing
character of war and security.[15]

Advocates of privatization argue, further, that the private military/
security industry can often perform vital military tasks – particularly in cases of humanitarian intervention – far more efficiently
and in more cost-effective and politically achievable fashion
than traditional UN or coalition forces.[16] While the debate goes
on, the industry is increasing its market share of conflict zones
through involvement in such conflicts as those in Afghanistan,
the Democratic Republic of Congo, Iraq and Sudan.

Despite the increasing demand for the services that are provided by the private military/security industry, the fact remains

that in modern times contracted combatants have been almost universally considered to be morally problematic. Surprisingly, however, there has been very little scholarly exploration of just what it is that so tarnishes the character of the private warrior. What seems to have been lost amidst the cloud of emotional accusations, counter-accusations and controversy over the specifics of companies like Blackwater and Executive Outcomes, is the capacity for clear and rational analysis of a range of broader and more fundamental questions about contracted combatants. What exactly, if anything, justifies the widely held view that these 'private warriors' (as we might also refer to them) are morally objectionable? Are there any conditions under which the contracted combatant might be considered to be on a moral par with his or her counterpart in national military service? Can a private warrior genuinely display the warrior virtues? What, if anything, accounts for the widespread intuition that armed contractors are intrinsically unreliable and untrustworthy? To call someone a mercenary is unquestionably one of the more offensive descriptions we can give of a fellow human being. But what, exactly, is it about this kind of activity which validates such moral censure? This book is an attempt to address these and other relevant issues which fall broadly into the category of the ethics of armed conflict.

Among the earliest of the handful of modern philosophical treatments of the moral status of contracted combatants is a book chapter by one of Australia's most well known philosophers, the University of Melbourne's C. A. J. (Tony) Coady.[17] There Coady points out that we can easily imagine a group of private warriors working together as 'Just Warriors, Inc.', who take remuneration for their services but who only offer those services in support of just causes. In this book I seek to explore in depth the question of what conceptual conditions would need to be met to make 'Just Warriors, Inc.' a reality. My central thesis can be articulated in the form of a play on Coady's idea of 'Just Warriors, Inc.', hence the title of this book. In essence I argue that contracted combatants are 'just' (merely, simply) warriors, not significantly different in kind from their counterparts serving in their nations' uniformed services. I argue further that the conditions which determine whether or not contracted combatants are 'Just' (moral/ethical) participants in armed hostilities are much the same conditions which determine whether or not soldiers, sailors, airmen and marines are themselves 'Just Warriors'.

It must be stressed from the very beginning that this is a work of philosophical enquiry, aiming to explore and address what are fundamentally conceptual questions. As a consequence, while questions of empirical fact do inform my argument, this is by no means a treatise on the nature of today's private military/security industry, the status of existing legal provisions governing the rights and responsibilities of armed contractors, or anything of that sort. In fact, this book deliberately explores a possibility which is not meaningfully on the cards in the current political climate, namely the employment of contracted combatants in fully fledged combat roles. There are no meaningful suggestions from companies in this industry that this is a role they are seeking – to the contrary, companies that work in this general field are careful to emphasize that they offer only 'defensive' guarding and protection services. So why the broader focus of this book? The goal of this book is to explore the fundamental conceptual issues relevant to the use of armed force by private contractors. To explore these in any depth – to consider the implications of contract *warriors* – requires addressing the issue without being constrained by the existing political, legal and public climate.

In focusing on contracted combatants I am leaving aside the majority of the services which companies within the private military and security industry provide, from training and advisory services, to landmine clearance, surveillance and intelligence analysis. In so doing I do not intend to suggest that there are no ethical issues raised by these activities. To the contrary, I am convinced that there are a range of interesting and challenging issues to be addressed here. For example, the respected Israeli military ethicist, Professor Asa Kasher has argued that military training should not be left in the hands of private contractors because of concerns over what he calls 'interface ethics', the issue of whether there is a sufficient degree of 'fit' between the ethics imparted by the trainer, on the one hand, and the ethics of the military force to which the trainee belongs, on the other.[18] I do not set these issues aside because they are uninteresting or unimportant, but only because space does not allow. For the same reason, I do not here attend to other intriguing questions like whether or not there might be some circumstances under which the employment of contracted combatants by private individuals or groups might be justified (for example, if an individual with the personal fortune of a Bill Gates contracted a private company to provide combatants to intervene in order to stop a genocide). I focus here specifically on the employment of contracted combatants by *states*, and leave aside these other issues to be addressed elsewhere.

In what follows I begin, in Chapter 1, by giving a description of the central features which account for the moral esteem in which most people hold military personnel. I identify what might be broadly referred to as the 'warrior virtues', namely courage (both moral and physical), comradeship, sense of honour, sacrifice and professionalism. In Chapter 2 I consider the question 'What the heck is a mercenary anyway?' and conclude that this derisive term and others like it (including 'whores of war') are inadequate to the task of describing the moral status of contracted combatants, and are best dispensed with. In Chapter 3 I draw on the description of the virtuous warrior set out in Chapter 1 to assess whether there are any intrinsic reasons why a private warrior could not also fulfil the requirements of a virtuous warrior. I argue that there are no flaws which apply generally to the character of all private warriors, such that they are by nature unable to display courage, exhibit comradeship and a sense of discipline, or lack an appropriate sense of honour. The different role of the contracted combatant means that the virtue of sacrifice is not one that can legitimately be expected to be among his moral characteristics, but I argue that this fact does not dishonour the private warrior.

In Chapter 4 I consider the fundamental basis of a state's 'right to fight', which is derived from the implicit contract that exists between the state and its citizens. Drawing on philosophical accounts of the social contract, I argue that the employment of contracted combatants by the state does not violate the state's monopoly on force and that the 'right to fight' can extend to private warriors. Chapter 5 continues this theme by considering the subservience of the military to the democratically elected government that is a moral consequence of the social contract. This relationship is generally referred to as 'civil–military relations', and the dominant theory of civil–military relations is that developed by the great political scientist Samuel Huntington. I argue, however, that a recent refinement of civil–military relations theory, namely the Agency Theory developed by Duke University's Peter Feaver, offers a more sophisticated understanding of civil–military relations that better accounts for the strategic relationship that exists between elected civilians and their military agents.

In Chapter 6 I examine the question of how contracted combatants fare when considered through the lens of Agency Theory. I contend that contracted combatants do not represent an intrinsic threat to this dimension of the democratic control of armed force. In fact, from a broadly conceptual perspective, it appears that not only do private military companies and state military forces share a fundamentally similar relationship with civilian principals, but on some counts private military companies also fare slightly better (from the perspective of the civilian principal) within that relationship.

Chapter 7 picks up from the preceding chapter by moving on from the general strategic relationship between elected civilians and military forces, to consider the issues of control and monitoring. After evaluating the means by which states monitor and control their armed forces, I then contend that these same or similar mechanisms are also available to states to ensure control over contracted combatants. In the final two chapters I turn to consider the appropriateness or otherwise of employing private warriors for humanitarian interventions and stability operations under an international mandate. Chapter 8 is dedicated to outlining James Pattison's comprehensive 'moderate instrumentalist approach' to the question of who should intervene in response to circumstances of extreme humanitarian crisis. In Chapter 9 I argue (contra Pattison) that contracted combatants fare well in the light of Pattison's framework, and that there are in fact reasons to consider contracted combatants to be sometimes more suitable for humanitarian interventions than state military forces.

Before continuing, a brief note on terminology is in order. In Chapter 2, as mentioned, I contend that the term 'mercenary' and other similar terms of negative connotation are unhelpful and unwarranted when considering persons who contract to perform military services. I have, therefore, coined the phrase 'contracted combatant' as a neutral alternative, and use this interchangeably with the terms 'private warrior' and 'armed contractor'. I also generally refer to the companies that provide the services of these individuals as 'private military companies' or PMCs. I am aware that, in so doing, I am going against the current academic trend (which is to refer to private military/security companies, or PMSCs) and am using a term disliked by the industry itself. Given that this book is focused on the ethical ramifications of the (largely hypothetical) idea of using contractors in direct combat roles in contemporary conflicts, the terminology seems nonetheless apt. Finally, because both the military profession and the private military industry are generally still male dominated (particularly in combat roles), I tend to make use of the male pronoun here. I do not by this intend in any way to belittle or ignore the often impressive contributions of the women warriors who serve in today's military forces or as contracted combatants.

1   On Sheepdogs (or, the Warrior's Honour)

We sleep soundly in our beds at night because rough men stand ready to do violence on our behalf.

Winston Churchill (attributed)

In his book *On Combat*, retired US Army Ranger Lt Col Dave Grossman recounts a conversation he once had with an old soldier. The soldier, a retired colonel and Vietnam veteran, shared with Grossman his view that society is divided into three basic categories. Most people, he contended, are **sheep**. 'They are kind, gentle, productive creatures who can only hurt one another by accident.' These ordinary average people face a threat, however, from those who occupy the next societal class: the **wolves**. 'The wolves feed on the sheep without mercy,' continued Grossman's companion. But they, in turn, are confronted by the third group, the **sheepdogs**. It was in this last category that the old warrior counted himself as a member. 'I'm a sheepdog. I live to protect the flock and confront the wolf.'[1]

Grossman's recounting and exegesis of this veteran's wisdom has struck a resounding chord with many who serve in the military, police and other security services. The old warrior's parable seems to them to simply, yet profoundly, capture the essence of their purpose. For those who serve in the armed forces the parable stands as a reminder to them that, though violence is the underpinning of their professions, the way of the warrior is an *honourable* path.

There are of course those who disagree, those who hold instead to the view that violence is never justifiable. While this is a minority view, and not one that will be addressed in this book, the basic intuition on which it stands is nonetheless one that must be taken seriously by all. For there can be no question that violence, and particularly the killing of fellow human beings, is an evil. Were we to find ourselves in some ideal world in which violence and killing were entirely absent, we should think it particularly deviant should someone view that absence as a loss.

Pacifists aside, however, it is generally accepted that under certain circumstances violence and killing are justifiable. Furthermore, there is a widespread belief that those who protect and serve society using, where necessary, controlled and sometimes deadly force, do not suffer dishonour for doing so. To the contrary, there is a strong and widely shared intuition that these warriors, as we shall call them here, are in some way worthy of greater honour than the average 'sheep'.

Just what is it that accounts for this intuition? What, in other words, is the basis for the warrior's honour? This perennial question must be answered repeatedly both for the sake of society at large and for the warriors themselves. As military ethicist Martin Cook points out, 'Morally conscientious military personnel need to understand and frame their actions in moral terms so as to maintain moral integrity in the midst of the actions and stress of combat. They do so in order to explain to themselves and others how the killing of human beings they do is distinguishable from the criminal act of murder.'[2]

In what follows in this chapter I will outline the central reasons that account for the esteem in which, it seems to me, the warrior is properly held. For the purposes of this chapter I shall take the term 'warrior' to refer to what we might take as the paradigm cases – the soldiers, marines, airmen and sailors who serve their country in the face of determined and violent enemies. I do not, however, intend to suggest that there are not others who deserve the title of warrior. To the contrary it seems fairly obvious that, for example, many police officers could rightly be called warriors, at least in the sense in which the idea of a warrior is interchangeable with the sheepdog in the parable mentioned above. And it would be hard to deny that the ordinary citizens aboard United Airlines Flight 93 displayed the courage and self-sacrifice characteristic of the warrior when they took on their hijackers on 11 September 2001 ('let's roll'). However, because the goal of this book is to assess whether there is a place for armed contractors in today's armed conflicts, and the obvious point of comparison is with the member of a national military force, I will restrict the term warrior here to the narrow sense applicable to that comparative exercise.

THE WARRIOR VIRTUES

As military ethicist Shannon French points out, 'When they are trained for war, warriors are given a mandate by their society to take lives. But they must learn to take only certain lives in certain ways, at certain times, and for certain reasons. Otherwise, they become indistinguishable from murderers and will find them- selves condemned by the very societies they were created to serve.'[3] Part of the reason that the warrior is due honour and not condemnation is because of the role he or she plays in defend- ing the citizens of the state to which he or she belongs. This is an issue I address later in this book. However, before turning to what we might think of as external factors such as this (external, that is, to the warrior's character), it makes sense to begin by consider- ing what the virtues of the individual soldier, marine, airman or sailor are which make him worthy of our respect. To return for a moment to the sheepdog analogy, what are the characteristics that the 'true' warrior shows that are equivalent to the courage, patience, endurance and loyalty which make the sheepdog such an admirable creature?

What follows is no more than a sketch of an answer to this important question. A full response would require a book of its own, and is more than is required for our purposes here. I have deliberately tried to describe the virtuous warrior in a manner with which most ethicists and military personnel would (I hope) agree, and have steered away from the contentious philosophical debates at the fringes of this description. I have also used the term 'virtue' somewhat loosely, and mean the term to reflect everyday usage rather than strict philosophical definition. Some of what I describe below are probably more properly called characteristics rather than virtues, but they are morally positive characteristics and I hope my (mis)use of the term 'virtue' conveys this and does not distract from the description. I also hope it is obvious that what is sketched below is an ideal which real people strive to achieve, rather than a description of a group of moral super-beings. This sketch does, nonetheless, reflect the inescapable fact that the unique challenges which arise in the circumstances of armed conflict call for men and women of high ethical calibre to engage with them. As General Sir John Hackett once said, 'A man can be selfish, cowardly, disloyal, false, fleeting, perjured, and morally corrupt in a wide variety of other ways and still be outstandingly good in pursuits in which other imperatives bear than those upon the fighting man. He can be a superb creative artist, for example, or a scientist in the very top flight, and still be a very bad man. What the bad man cannot be is a good sailor, or soldier, or airman.'[4]

Courage

On 28 June 2005, Lt Michael P. Murphy and the three other members of his US Navy SEAL reconnaissance team were in the rugged mountains of Konar Province, on the Afghan side of the Afghanistan-Pakistan border. Their mission: to locate one of the key leaders of the insurgency being conducted against the Afghan government and coalition forces in Afghanistan. Despite the considerable skills of Lt Murphy and his team, a local goat herder stumbled upon their surveillance position. Murphy was faced with a quandary: should he give the order to kill the goat herder, thereby giving his team the time necessary to relocate to a safer hiding spot, or should he allow the herder to live and risk discovery by Taliban insurgents located in the vicinity? Together with his team-mates, Murphy decided on the latter course of action.

Shortly thereafter, their position was besieged by an estimated 30 to 40 insurgents. A brutal fire-fight ensued in which numerous enemy fighters were killed or wounded. All four members of the heavily outnumbered SEAL team were also wounded, and despite numerous attempts they were unable to reach their headquarters on the radio to call for support. When the team's radio operator fell mortally wounded, Murphy continued trying to get through, eventually concluding that the extreme terrain in which their fighting position was located made radio contact impossible. Without hesitation Murphy left his team-mates and fought his way to open terrain where he was finally able to call for help. His exposed position left him extremely vulnerable to enemy fire. Nonetheless he continued to engage the enemy until (as he must surely have expected) he was mortally wounded. For his selfless leadership and extraordinary courage Lt Murphy was posthumously awarded the Medal of Honor, the highest military decoration awarded by the government of the United States. The sole surviving member of the four-man team and Murphy's best friend, Marcus Luttrell, described him as an 'iron-souled warrior of colossal, almost unbelievable courage.'[5]

There can be little question that courage, as so remarkably demonstrated by Lt Murphy, is the queen of the military virtues. Though courage on its own does not make a warrior, the idea of a true warrior who lacks courage is inconceivable. This multi-faceted virtue is one I must, therefore, give due consideration to here.

Although Aristotle's ideas on courage (primarily in his *Nichomachean Ethics*) have been described as 'a pit of quicksand' and in some ways 'frustratingly implausible',[6] it is nonetheless his thoughts which are usually taken as the starting point for discussions of this virtue. Peter Olsthoorn reflects an uncontentious reading of Aristotle's view of courage when he describes it as 'the middle position between rashness and cowardice',[7] and 'having the right attitude concerning feelings of confidence and fear in the pursuance of a morally just cause'.[8] Unlike Plato who, in his *Laches*, sought to apply the idea of courage very broadly,[9] Aristotle saw it as a virtue with particular application to the military profession, and viewed the paradigm case of the brave man as 'someone who does not fear a noble death in war'.[10]

Like many virtues, courage is not comfortably reducible to elements which can be subjected to scientific analysis. Most scientific studies that do attempt to study this phenomenon limit their definition of courage to something like acting positively while experiencing fear. But while there are some advantages to viewing courage in this way, what is left out is the critical aspect of motivation. The distinction between physical courage and moral courage is important here. As Olsthoorn puts it, 'Whereas the word "physical" in the term physical courage refers to what is at stake, life and limbs, the word "moral" in the term moral courage refers to the higher end that this form of courage aims at.'[11] Aristotle seems to view courage as a combination of both, requiring the willingness to risk (where necessary) physical harm in the service of the noble end. Lt Murphy's actions provide a remarkable example of this combination – he displayed a firm and sacrificial commitment to the 'noble end' in his refusal to kill the goat herder, which led in turn to the circumstances in which he exhibited extraordinary physical courage in seeking to protect his comrades.

Though it seems likely that those with moral courage are also likely to be physically courageous when the need arises, it is useful to see both facets of this virtue because while it is physical courage that is most recognized in the military (through, for example, the awarding of medals[12]), it is in fact moral courage which is more regularly demanded of warriors, particularly when it takes the form of *integrity*. James Toner writes that 'Integrity – knowing what to be – is the hallmark of the skilled officer, for character and competence . . . are complementary.'[13] The willingness to do what one holds to be right, even in the face of disapproval and opposition from among one's peers, is critical for ensuring the virtue of as tribal a group as the military. Though it sometimes sits in tension with another key warrior virtue, that of *duty*, this is a necessary tension even where it creates problems for military organizations (as in the case of selective conscientious objectors, those who have volunteered for military service but who refuse to participate in particular wars on ethical grounds).[14] Individual integrity acts as a vital brake to the potential excesses which can arise from the over-application of the military norm of obedience to authority (*Semper Fidelis*). The latter norm, if unchecked, can lead to excesses or even atrocities on the battlefield and, less dramatically but also importantly, abusive behavior within military units. But integrity itself must be kept in its proper place. Paul Robinson writes that integrity 'should be viewed as an Aristotelian mean flanked by excesses such as arrogance and deficiencies such as weakness of will'.[15]

Moral courage is, therefore, critical. At the same time, however, it is the physical dimension of courage that makes this distinctly a warrior virtue. All kinds of people – lawyers, accountants, teachers and so on – are required on occasion to show moral courage, but few other professions demand the physical courage which is so intrinsic to the traditional understanding of warriorhood.

I say 'traditional understanding' here because several important contemporary commentators have argued that, in the Western world at least, the traditional virtues which have defined the warrior caste have eroded, and have been replaced by an occupational or economic view of the military profession.[16] In this 'post-heroic' age, argue eminent scholars like Christopher Coker,[17] war has become 'disenchanted'[18] and the value of virtues like courage have been displaced by a focus on technical expertise, as Western nations become increasingly squeamish about taking casualties on the battlefield and go to extraordinary lengths to ensure 'force protection'. As the concern for community has over time become replaced by the individual in Western societies,[19] so the argument goes, so traditional motivations to serve in the military (indeed, even the notion of military 'service' itself) have declined and been replaced by individualist motivations such as career advancement, salary and thrill seeking. This is a theme which will demand our attention several times in the course of this book. For now it is enough to note the existence of such claims before moving on.

Comradeship

While courage is the key individual virtue that defines the warrior, the true warrior is not a lone wolf. While he may sometimes, even often, have to act on his own, the warrior is almost always part of a team, and the bond of comradeship he forms with the other members of that team is a critical part of his identity. It is a commonplace that military service, and particularly the crucible of combat, forms bonds between warriors which are arguably unmatched in the civilian world. These bonds can be a significant factor when it comes to combat motivation, as attested to in this moving passage penned by William Manchester regarding his Second World War military experience:

> I understand, at last, why I jumped hospital that Sunday thirty-five years ago and, in violation of orders, returned to the front and almost certain death. It was an act of love. Those men on the line were my family, my home. They were closer to me than I can say, closer than any friends had been or ever would be. They had never let me down, and I couldn't do it to them. I had to be with them, rather than let them die and me live with the knowledge that I might have saved them. Men, I now knew, do not fight for flag or country, for the Marine Corps

or glory or any other abstraction. They fight for one another. Any man in combat who lacks comrades who will die for him, or for whom he is willing to die, is not a man at all. He is truly damned.[20]

The motivational potential of comradeship – or, to use the more morally neutral term, *cohesion* – is well recognized by military forces, and considerable effort is made to use training, unit structures and cultures to reinforce its power. It is no surprise, for example, that the US Marine Corps' advertising slogan ('The Few. The Proud') so closely mirrors the words which Shakespeare put into the mouth of King Henry V in the famous St Crispin's Day oratory:

> This story shall the good man teach his son;
> And Crispin Crispian shall ne'er go by,
> From this day to the ending of the world,
> But we in it shall be remember'd;
> We few, we happy few, we band of brothers;
> For he to-day that sheds his blood with me
> Shall be my brother; be he ne'er so vile,
> This day shall gentle his condition:
> And gentlemen in England now a-bed
> Shall think themselves accursed they were not here,
> And hold their manhoods cheap whiles any speaks
> That fought with us upon Saint Crispin's day.[21]

Who could fail to be stirred by these words? They strike a chord deep within, somewhere in the very nature of our humanity. If we do find ourselves jaded in the light of such talk, it must surely be more a reaction to Hollywood's exploitation of our emotions in this regard rather than any lack of genuine resonance. There is, however, a negative dimension of cohesion or comradeship which must be recognized. Sometimes it is fear and not courage that comradeship encourages, fear of being ostracized or shunned from the all-important group. Physical courage can be motivated by the fear of shame, which for some can be an even greater fear than the fear of death. Olsthoorn's reminder is therefore important: 'If an act of courage does not meet the Aristotelian requirement of noble intention . . . but is motivated by the wish to gain esteem or save face instead, it is not very likely to be motivated by moral courage.'[22]

While military institutions are heavily invested in the idea that it is the personal bonds between members of units which serve as a key motivator in combat (the idea that 'each man fights for the man next to him'), it is interesting to note that there is a growing body of research which suggests that interpersonal bonds are not as important as is generally believed in securing optimum performance. There seems in fact to be good reason to believe that task cohesion (a shared commitment to the same goals), rather than unit cohesion *per se*, has a stronger correlation with mission success.[23] This is perhaps not all that surprising, given the feelings of comradeship which many military personnel have towards other warriors who they've never met but who have served in the same or similar operational environments.

Closely related to cohesion is *discipline*. Discipline is, obviously, a virtue which applies to individuals, but it has its greatest application in the context of a group, and arguably the military context sees the pinnacle of its relevance. Field Marshal William Slim once made this point well when he wrote, 'The more modern war becomes, the more essential appear the basic qualities that from the beginning of history have distinguished armies from mobs. The first of these is discipline.'[24] While discipline is in part a product of drill and training, that 'muscle memory' that kicks in when orders are shouted or contact is made with the enemy, it is certainly also more than that. Again Field Marshal Slim is helpful here, in his eloquent account of the connection between comradeship and discipline: 'the real discipline that a man holds to . . . is a refusal to betray his comrades. The discipline that makes a sentry, whose whole body is tortured for sleep, rest his chin on the point of his bayonet because he knows, if he nods, he risks the lives of the men sleeping behind him.'[25]

Sense of Honour

> . . . *if it be a sin to covet honour, I am the most offending soul alive.*
>
> *Henry V*, Act 4, Scene 3

Honour is a notion which seems distinctly old-fashioned to most moderns, yet it has long been considered a critical aspect of the self-identity of military personnel. According to a widely quoted definition, 'honour is the value of a person in his own eyes, but also in the eyes of his society. It is his estimation of his own worth, his claim to pride, but it is also the acknowledgement of that claim, his excellence recognized by society, his right to pride.'[26] Though sometimes treated as one, honour is not itself a virtue. Instead, as Aristotle pointed out, honour is the reward for virtue, and it is the sense or love of honour (*philotimia*) that is the virtue itself.[27]

Though archaic sounding to modern ears, valuing honour has a long and distinguished history. The Roman philosopher Marcus Tullius Cicero defended honour against its Stoic and Epicurean detractors, and in so doing developed a highly sophisticated and compelling account thereof. As late as the seventeenth century, Francis Bacon wrote that 'There is an *Honour* (. . .), which may be ranked among the Greatest, which happenth rarely: That is, of such as *Sacrifice themselves,* to *Death* or *Dangers,* for the *Good* of their *Countrey*.'[28]

But this positive view of honour was significantly eroded by the onset of the Enlightenment. Philosophers like Hobbes, Bentham, and Locke were midwives to a radical societal change in which human beings were viewed primarily as creatures of self-interest. The concept of honour fell foul of this radical new outlook. As Quentin Skinner eloquently put it: 'With his bristling code of honor and his continual thirst for glory, the typical hero of the Renaissance began to appear slightly comical in his wilful disregard for the natural instinct of self-preservation.'[29] More than this, the Enlightenment's firm rejection of pride made the quest for honour something to be despised. Even after more than 270 years, it is impossible not to hear the sneer in the Enlightenment thinker Bernard Mandeville's voice when he wrote that '. . . pride has nowhere been more encouraged than in the army' and 'never anything has been invented before, that was half so effective to create artificial courage among military men'.[30]

We now have enough distance from their time to see that the purely economic view of humanity they were so strongly committed to gives, in some respects, a distorted view of human nature. In their quest for realism they ironically rejected the quintessentially pragmatic and realist views of thinkers like Cicero. As Peter Olsthoorn explains:

> In Cicero's view, soldiers, although far from selfish, cannot be expected to perform their duties from a sense of duty alone. Both inside and outside the sphere of war, only the perfectly wise act virtuously for virtue's sake. However, those perfectly wise are rare – Cicero himself claimed that he had never met such a person. . . . For the not so wise, that is, most of us, a little help from the outside, consisting of the judgements of our peers and our concern for our reputation, can be of help. The censure from our peers is a punishment we cannot escape and, more importantly, no one is insensible enough to put up with the blame of others – that is a burden too heavy to bear. Virtuous persons are, in general, far from indifferent to praise, and this should not be held against them. Those who on the other hand claim to be insensitive to fame and glory are not to be believed.[31]

The economic view of humanity ushered in by the Enlightenment seems at first blush to fit comfortably enough with the contemporary trend away from citizen armies to military forces made up entirely of volunteers – the 'All Volunteer Force' (AVF), in US military parlance. Renowned military sociologist Charles Moskos has argued that the move to the AVF signalled a shift in emphasis in the US military from being a 'calling', with the focus being on service and sacrifice, to being an occupation or career, in which self-interest began to take on a more central role.[32] But while there is truth in this analysis, its implications can be exaggerated. For while it is certainly true that the introduction of the AVF has seen an increase in the professionalism of the US military (and other military forces which have followed this route), this has not had the feared effect that 'bland careerism' has robbed members of the military of the higher commitments that have tradition- ally characterized their historical counterparts. The pecuniary and careerist focus that is, undeniably, part of the AVF, does not adequately account for the commendable behaviour of the majority of those men and women who have served in recent times in places like Bosnia, Somalia, Afghanistan and Iraq. A sense of honour remains a critical motivating force for today's warriors. The desire for honour seems to tap into something deep in the human psyche. Indeed, 'The concern for external validation may even be hardwired into human biology.'[33] As Christopher Coker puts it, 'What we desire, above all else, is respect, and it is through the warrior's conduct in battle that respect is won.'[34]

In her book *The Code of the Warrior: Exploring Warrior Values Past and Present,* Shannon French points out that the desire for honour is one which can be identified in a wide range of cultures and military traditions throughout history, and that this usually results in the development of some form of warrior code. Beyond this, she argues, 'most warriors also feel themselves a part of an even longer line, a line of men and women from diverse cultures throughout history who are deserving of the label "warrior". This is a legacy that spans not just centuries but millennia.'[35]

Honour is not reducible to glory. While we certainly do respect the abilities and physical courage of those who display excep- tional prowess in battle, that on its own is not sufficient to earn honour. We can, for example, respect the fighting capabilities of some of the die-hard Nazis of the Second World War, without conferring upon them the status of 'honourable warrior'. As Michael Ignatieff has pointed out, the warrior's honour is also an ethic of responsibility: 'Wherever the art of war was practised, war- riors distinguished between combatants and non-combatants, legitimate and illegitimate targets, moral and immoral weaponry, civilized and barbarous usage in the treatment of prisoners and of the wounded. Such codes may have been honoured as often in the breach as in the observance, but without them war is not war – it is no more than slaughter.'[36] The warrior's honour, then, is not simply a spur to standing firm in battle, or displaying heroic courage, it is also the basis of *restraint* under the chaotic and taxing conditions imposed by armed conflict (and as such is a close companion of the moral courage discussed earlier). Here we might follow Paul Robinson's distinction between external and internal honour. External honour – the esteem in which a warrior is held by peers, family, friends and society – tends to be a strong motive for acts of courage. Internal honour – the esteem in which a warrior holds himself – is more often a motive for restraint in warfare, and is 'associated with virtues such as self-control and mercifulness'.[37]

Two examples help illustrate the point. During the war in Vietnam one young enlisted Marine was pushed by the stress of combat to the verge of committing an atrocity. An officer discovered the young man with his rifle held to the head of a Vietnamese woman. Instead of threatening the Marine with a court martial or something of that sort, the officer simply said 'Marines don't do that.' 'Jarred out of his berserk state and recalled to his place in a longstanding warrior tradition, the Marine stepped back and lowered his weapon.'[38] More recently, on 3 April 2005, a patrol of American soldiers were making their way through Najaf in Iraq when an angry crowd of several hundred shouting and fist-waving Iraqis emerged from the buildings on either side of the street and converged on the small group of soldiers. Conditions looked ripe for a violent confrontation, perhaps even a massacre:

> At that moment, an American officer stepped through the crowd holding his rifle high over his head with the barrel pointed to the ground. Against the backdrop of the seething crowd, it was a striking

gesture . . . 'Take a knee,' the officer said. . . . The soldiers looked at him as if he were crazy. Then, one after another, swaying in their bulky body armor and gear, they knelt before the boiling crowd and pointed their guns at the ground. The Iraqis fell silent, and their anger subsided. The officer ordered his men to withdraw [and continue on their patrol].[39]

The balance between the desire for external honour and internal honour is critical. The motivation towards courage which is provided by the desire for external honour is vital in the military profession, but there is a danger that those who put prime store in external honour will tend towards extremes. There is a fine line between courage and recklessness, and without the balancing provided by the restraints imposed by internal honour that line can all too easily be crossed, often at the cost of the lives of comrades. This is not to say that sacrifice will not sometimes be necessary, and it is to this that we now turn.

Sacrifice

The willingness to sacrifice life and limb when circumstances demand is perhaps the defining characteristic of the virtue of the warrior. General Sir John Hackett is often credited with being the first to explain this relationship in terms of a 'contract of unlimited liability'. The notion that the relationship between volunteer members of a nation's military and the society they serve is a form of contract (both legal *and* moral) is a very helpful one. As military ethicist Martin Cook puts it in the context of US military officers' service:

> The terms of the contract are that the military officer agrees to serve the government and people of the United States. He or she accepts the reality that military service may, under some circumstances, entail risk or loss of life in that service. This contract is justified in the mind of the officer because of the moral commitment to the welfare of the United States and its citizens.[40]

Christopher Coker makes the valuable point that sacrifice is not only a defining characteristic of the virtuous warrior; it is in fact a defining characteristic of war itself. Coker argues that it is sacrifice which transforms the violence of war from mere killing into something with a metaphysical meaning. 'It is sacrifice which makes war qualitatively different from every other act of violence. We rarely celebrate killing but we do celebrate dying when it has meaning, not only for the dead, but for those they leave behind.'[41]

The power of that metaphysical transformation cannot be underestimated. Here sacrifice is often tied to patriotism. Examples abound, I offer just one. Consider this statement by decorated war hero and former Republican Party presidential candidate, Senator John McCain:

> I believe that young men and women join the armed forces to serve a cause greater than self-interest. They must make the most of their patriotism. They must foster virtues of courage, obedience, loyalty, and conscientiousness. To have a military that functions as well as it can, it must be fully committed to endorsing these virtues and behaviors in military professionals. It requires a sense of honor that demands as the price of self-respect the sacrifice of self-interest. What a poor life it is that has no greater object than itself.
>
> Those who claim their liberty but not their duty to the civilization that ensures it live a half-life. Success, wealth, and celebrity gained and kept for private interest is a small thing. It makes us comfortable, eases the material hardships our children will bear, and purchases a fleeting regard for our lives, yet not the self-respect that in the end will matter to us most. But have the character to sacrifice for a cause greater than self-interest and invest in life with the eminence of that cause, and self-respect is assured.[42]

Professionalism

While warriors have not always been professionals, there is little question that professionalism is an essential aspect of the character of today's virtuous warrior. There is a vast literature on the nature of professions in general, and the military profession in particular, and I can do little more here than give a rough outline of the main issues. I will address this issue in more detail later in this book.

Historically it was only members of the officer class who were considered to belong to the military profession. This is because, since Revolutionary France revolutionized warfare through the introduction of the *levée en masse* in the late eighteenth century, most armies were made up primarily of conscripts, led and organized by a small core of career officers. This perception is, however, changing with the (relatively recent) advent of the All Volunteer Force, and military personnel of all ranks are increasingly being considered to be military professionals.

By far the most widely recognized definition of the military profession is that put forward by Samuel Huntington. Huntington's classic definition sees the professional soldier as being defined by three main characteristics: 'a politically neutral sense of duty to the state, military expertise and a professional identity'.[43]

The first of these characteristics is generally considered to be the most important of the three. In Western societies at least, the idea that the soldier is to serve the state *qua* state, and in so doing eschew party political agendas, is almost axiomatic. For the professional soldier, duty to the state is the virtue *summum bonum*. The move to the All Volunteer Force gave rise to concerns among some scholars that the 'occupational view' of the military would undermine this core value, but this seems not to have happened.[44]

The military professional is also defined by his or her unique expertise in the art of warfighting and its subservient elements. As Cook puts it, 'It is the essence of a profession that members possess unique knowledge and the skill to apply that knowledge to a given range or sphere of service.'[45] The ever increasing complexity of conventional manoeuvre warfare and its less glamorous relatives – counterinsurgency, peacekeeping and 'operations other than war' – have led to the emergence of an extensive range of military education and training opportunities for the modern professional soldier.

Against this, however, Krahmann contends that the growing use of civilian technologies by the military, and the increasing emphasis on technological know-how have in fact narrowed the distinctive set of skills of the modern warrior to those learned in basic combat training.[46] It might be added to this that the emergence of counterinsurgency as the dominant form of warfare (for now, at least) further decreases the distinctiveness of the military professional's area of competence, as in counterinsurgency kinetic warfighting skills are (or should be) kept to a minimum, while non-traditional skills such as training police, building local economies and administering humanitarian aid come to the fore.

But this viewpoint ignores the centrality of what military professionals call 'operational art' to all that they do. Effective military operations can only be undertaken by those who grasp this art, and it is by no means reducible to a set of technical skills. The true military professional is, therefore, not a military technician, but rather what Cook calls a 'soldier-scholar', someone who 'preserves both aspects of truly professional officership: excellence in performance of military skills as currently understood by the profession and the contribution as a scholar to the continuing evolution of the body of professional knowledge that advances the profession through time'.[47]

The third feature of the military professional, as identified by Huntington, is that of *identity*. This identity is, in part, defined by the unique body of knowledge which the military professional shares with his or her counterparts. But it is also far more than that. As Cook points out, when one enters a profession one also

> . . . learns the identity of a pantheon of archetypal members of the profession and stories of their contributions to the profession. One becomes familiar with a set of institutions, awards, honors, and so forth, that members of the profession know and value (and that

generally members outside the profession do not). One picks up, almost unconsciously, the small signals in dress, attitude, speech, and so forth that members use to signal to one another that they are members of the same professional group.[48]

The identity of the military profession is also defined *externally*, that is, by how the profession is viewed by society. Recognition as a profession is conveyed by society based on it being perceived as morally praise-worthy, worthy of confidence and respect, and (perhaps as a result) being vested with prestige.

CONCLUSION

We are now in a position to draw together a description of the virtuous warrior.

The warrior is a person of courage, both the physical courage to face the dangers of combat as well as the moral courage to stand firm in the face of illegal orders or peer pressure, and exercise restraint and discernment on the battlefield. He is strongly tied by the cords of comradeship to those he serves alongside (including those with whom he shares no direct personal relationship), and he has the discipline to play his part in ensuring the cohesion of his unit. He is, furthermore, characterized by a sense of honour. That is to say, he desires and seeks to be worthy of the esteem of the society he serves, while also seeking to stay true to his internal moral compass. The former motivates him to acts of courage on the battlefield, while the latter ensures that he exercises the restraint of a moral combatant. He is, above all, willing to sacrifice his life or physical well-being to serve his country. This does not, however, make him a fanatic. Instead, he is the quintessential professional. His commitment to the state he serves is politically neutral. He possesses and continues to expand the core expertise of the military profession. And he both identifies with, and is identified by society as a member of, the military profession.

All this has been by way of precursor to our true subject, the contracted combatant. Is the contracted combatant truly a warrior at all? Or is he a despicable mercenary, to be derided as a 'whore of war'? It is to these questions we now turn.

2   What the Heck is a Mercenary Anyway?

At last I am in China where I hope to be of some service to a people who are struggling to attain national unity and new life.

Claire Chennault, commander of the Flying Tigers, in his diary on 31 May 1937[1]

'Dogs of War'.[2] 'Mercenaries'. 'Whores of War'. All these and many other pejorative labels have been used in the popular media and even by some scholars to describe the armed contractors who have in recent times guarded VIPs, convoys, oil-pipelines and other installations in places like Iraq and Afghanistan. Some of the concerns raised by those who use these terms relate to issues which we might think of as consequentialist, for example worries about the impact of armed contractors on the state's monopoly on force, and the moral/legal accountability of these contractors (issues I will address in subsequent chapters). The labels themselves, however, are unquestionably directed at the *character* of the individuals concerned. Indeed, the presumption of the moral corruption of these contractors is widespread. Yet very little sustained thought has been given to what, precisely, is supposed to account for this strongly negative character assessment. In this chapter and the next I will consider the question of whether there is something intrinsically morally problematic about the private warrior, something that would make it wrong to become a private warrior even in a logically possible world in which the employment of private warriors led to overwhelmingly good consequences. As will become clear, it is my contention that the all-too-common, sweeping and unthinking condemnation of the private warrior's character is generally misplaced and inaccurate.

Perhaps the best place to start is by asking the question Doug Brooks, President of the IPOA (the leading trade body for the private security industry) often poses to hostile interlocutors: 'What the heck is a mercenary anyway?' It's a good question, for while the armed contractors at work today in places like Iraq and Afghanistan reject the label, it's important to consider the content of the term in order to be clear just what it is that they're being accused of. Historically, of course, mercenarism was a wide-spread practice until the rise of the Westphalian state. As Patricia Owens points out:

> Sovereignty involved the ability to extract wealth from populations through taxation and borrowing, and to regularize armed forces and policing functions by eliminating 'private', that is, non-regular armies, such as privateers and pirates. Through a slow and uneven process, mercenaries, privateers and pirates were edged out of the military business. It is well known that the Thirty Years War which culminated in the Treaty of Westphalia was fought with large numbers of merce-naries for what was understood to be primarily financial gain. Over time, European armies comprised of soldiers of fortune declined. By the nineteenth century, more centrally controlled people's armies had emerged – *regularized* armed forces, serviced by men supposedly committed to a national cause, not only financial gain; eventually 'good' states, as well as successful states, fought wars using their own people.[3]

If that's the history, the question remains just how to define mercenarism. As it turns out, Brooks' question is not an easy one to answer. Certainly legislators who have tried to address the 'scourge of mercenarism' have found the idea of a mercenary to be difficult to pin down.[4] In his attempt to address this ques-tion, philosopher Uwe Steinhoff considers what he describes as a typical definition (consonant with recent international agreements), one given by Francoise Hampson, according to which 'Mercenaries appear to have three essential characteristics. They are foreign, motivated principally by financial gain and use force, but not as regular members of the armed forces of a State.'[5]

The characteristics which distinguish a mercenary from a regular soldier, on this sort of account, can be specified in terms of affiliation, motivation, and organizational incorporation. But we need not concede too much here, for there are significant problems with defining a mercenary in this way. Steinhoff points to a number of apparent counter-examples to Hampson's definition (as we shall see below), where someone we would generally qualify as a mercenary lacks one or more of these distinguishing characteristics. Steinhoff therefore offers his own definition, which has it that

> A mercenary is a person who is contracted to provide military services to groups other than his own (in terms of nation, ethnic group, class, etc.) and is ready to deliver this service even if this involves taking part in hostilities. Which groups are relevant depends on the nature of the conflict.[6]

This definition is unusual in not defining mercenarism specifically in terms of the motive for monetary gain, as Hampson's definition clearly does. Certainly, for most people, it is this pecuniary aspect of mercenarism which immediately springs to mind as this profession's most morally problematic characteristic. But as Steinhoff points out:

> If one looks at what are considered paradigmatic examples of mercenaries, for example the men of the Free companies or 'Mad' Mike Hoare's and Bob Denard's men in the Congo in the 1960s or 'Colonel' Callan in Angola in the 70s, it becomes very clear that these men, or at least a very significant number of them, were *not* motivated principally by financial gain (which does not mean that they were not at all motivated by financial gain), but [rather] by adventurism or a love for war and fighting.[7]

Of course money is not irrelevant here, hence the idea of contract in Steinhoff's definition. As Steinhoff explains:

> The financial motive, to be sure, should remain part of the definition of 'mercenary'. Someone who fights for free or for relatively small pay in war after war is a *pure* adventurer or a war junkie, not a mercenary. On the other hand, the financial motive does not need to override or dominate all others, not even moral or ideological ones. Mercenaries who fight exclusively in wars that meet certain moral or ideological preconditions are not only conceivable but real.[8]

An excellent example of what Steinhoff has in mind here are the American pilots of the 'Flying Tigers', or the American Volunteer Airgroup (AVG), under the command of the legendary Captain Claire L. Chennault, who fought for China against Japan prior to US entry into the Second World War. Flying Tigers pilots were US Army Air Corps, US Navy and US Marine Corps pilots who resigned their commissions in order to sign one-year contracts with the Central Aircraft Manufacturing Company, to 'manufacture, repair and operate aircraft'. They were well paid (earning up to $750 per month, a significant sum in that time) and had the added incentive of a $500 bonus for each Japanese aircraft they shot down. The financial motive was, therefore, a very real one, but it is also clear that many, if not most, of these 'mercenaries' were also motivated by such things as a love of adventure and the desire to help defeat Japanese aggression. In their Curtiss P40 Tomahawks, the colourful characters of the AVG became one of the most effective fighter units in the China-Burma-India theatre, accounting for an estimated 300 enemy aircraft. For many back home in the US the men of the Flying Tigers were heroes, avenging the attack on Pearl Harbor. That positive assessment has continued to the current day.[9] According to Pamela Feltus,

> In 1991, the Department of Veterans Affairs credited AVG service as time served with the U.S. armed services. The pilots were awarded the Distinguished Flying Cross, and the technicians and staff were

given the Bronze Star. After almost half a century, the first Americans to fight the Japanese were finally being recognized. They were mercenaries, gamblers, idealists, bar brawlers, and adventurers; but most importantly, the men of the AVG were patriots.[10]

Steinhoff's definition gives us a useful enough starting point in answering Doug Brooks' question ('what the heck is a mercenary anyway?'). But it does not go far enough. For there can be little question that the term 'mercenary' is a term of moral condemnation. But there seems nothing inherent in Steinhoff's definition that explains just what is *wrong* with being a mercenary. Wherein, exactly, lies the badness? As mentioned, very little has in fact been written in answer to this question. Notable among the few exceptions are a paper written by Anthony Coady and a paper jointly authored by Tony Lynch and Adrian Walsh.[11] Both papers take as their starting point Niccolo Machiavelli's comments on mercenaries in his famous and controversial work, *The Prince*.

According to Coady, Lynch and Walsh, Machiavelli's objections to mercenaries were effectively threefold:

1. Mercenaries are not sufficiently bloodthirsty.
2. Mercenaries cannot be trusted because of the temptations of political power.
3. There exists some motive or motives appropriate to engaging in war which mercenaries necessarily lack, or else mercenaries are motivated by some factor which is inappropriate to engaging in war.

The first of these points need not detain us long. For it is quite clear that, even if the empirically questionable claim that mercenaries lack the killing instinct necessary for war were true, this can hardly be considered a *moral* failing. But perhaps the point is instead one about effectiveness – the claim that the soldier for hire cannot be relied upon to do what is necessary in battle when the crunch comes, because he is too squeamish perhaps, or, in the terms we have been using in the previous chapter, because he lacks *courage*. This is certainly a concern which has been raised by those who have in recent times opposed the use of contractors in Iraq. As Mark Cancian, a retired US Marine Corps Colonel, Harvard graduate and Iraq veteran writes:

> . . . one of the great fears about reliance on contractors has been that contractors would prove unreliable under stress. Critics have cited Machiavelli's warning that 'mercenaries . . . are useless . . . without discipline, faithless . . .'. Fortunately, such dire warnings have not proven true. Contractors have continued to do their jobs under even the most dangerous and austere conditions.[12]

Cancian is here referring to contractors in general, not specifically the armed contractors who are the focus of this work. But, as will become clear in the next chapter, there is real evidence that armed contractors have also displayed courage in the face of danger.

This concern about the reliability of mercenaries seems to be in part inspired by the fact that mercenaries are usually defined as foreigners, as we have already noted. We might ask whether this is really an intrinsic feature of what it means to be a mercenary (if, indeed, this notion stands up under scrutiny at all). For why couldn't a state contractually employ a mercenary who happens to be one of that state's own citizens, but who, perhaps by some personality flaw, lacks patriotism or any particular tie of affection to his country or the people in it? Would such a person be somehow intrinsically more reliable than a foreigner, due to the particular colour of his passport? The flip side of this issue is that it seems an interesting argument could be made for the view that states ought *always* to prefer foreign mercenaries to citizen soldiers, for if the state has a duty to protect its citizens then that duty must surely extend also to those citizens who happen to make up the nation's armed forces. Thomas More makes exactly this point in articulating the strategies of his wise Utopians.[13]

Certainly, only the most radical cosmopolitan thinker would attempt to contest the claim that 'The virtuous state must favor its own citizens.'[14]

Even if Machiavelli's warning about the unreliability of mercenaries turned out to be true, it is evident this cannot be the moral failing we are looking for. For while we might cast moral aspersions on such a mercenary, those aspersions would be in the family of such terms as 'feeble', 'pathetic', or 'hopeless'. But these are quite clearly not the moral failings we are looking for in trying to discover just what is morally wrong with being a *mercenary*. Indeed, this very characteristic might just as easily be considered an ethically positive one. A more positive version of Machiavelli's claim, as Coady points out,[15] is that the mercenary may be less prone to the passions which lead the national or ethnic zealot soldier to demonize the enemy and seek their total destruction.

The second point is even more easily dealt with. For it is quite clear that the temptation to grab power over a nation by force is at least as strong for national military forces as it is for mercenaries. In fact, it could well be argued that mercenaries are more reliable in this respect, given that they are often foreign and therefore have less incentive to try to gain power over the nation that has contracted their services. A recent comprehensive analysis of coup trends in Africa between 1956 and 2001 addressed 80 successful coups, 108 unsuccessful coup attempts, and 139 reported coup plots. No discernable trend was reported of mercenaries being involved in coup attempts or coup plots. The only coup plots mentioned in the survey as involving mercenaries (an inadequate number to constitute a trend) were those involving Frenchman Bob Denard in the Comoros Islands (four of a total of at least 19 coups and attempted coups that occurred in those troubled islands between independence in 1975 and 2001).[16] Regardless of how telling this empirical point is, it seems clear that there is nothing about being a mercenary which makes one *more* susceptible to being tempted by the lure of political power that is not also a factor for a member of a national military force or equivalent. Again, this point simply does not give us a useful way of making a clear distinction between the positive moral status of the state warrior and the (presumed) negative moral standing of the mercenary.

The question of motives, however, is a weightier one, and requires more of our attention. The most common version of this objection is that there is something wrong with fighting for money. As pointed out above, it is a central feature of the definition of a mercenary that he be contracted to provide military services – he is not simply a volunteer, for mercenarism has an inescapable commercial dimension to it. James Pattison suggests that there are two general features of financial motivation that make it problematic: 'First, the financial motive is individualistic (at best it includes family members). Second, in extreme cases it suggests an amoral approach, and, in particular, indicates few limits on what one might do for personal gain.'[17]

As Lynch and Walsh point out, however, the objection cannot simply be that money is in itself a morally questionable motivator for action. For while a case could perhaps be made for this, it would apply to such a wide range of human activities that it offers little help in discerning what singles out mercenarism as especially problematic. Perhaps, therefore, the problem is being motivated by money above all else. Lynch and Walsh helpfully suggest that we label such a person a *lucrepath*. Certainly we do find something deeply objectionable about someone for whom the accumulation of money is always the overriding consideration. By this thinking, as Lynch and Walsh put it, 'Those criticizing mercenaries for taking blood money are then accusing them of being lucrepaths . . . it is not that they do things for money, but that money is the *sole* or the *dominant* consideration in their practical deliberations.'[18] This idea neatly captures the broader usage of the term mercenary when used beyond the context of 'soldiers for hire'. It also seems to fit with Pattison's concerns – he directs his reader's attention to those who are 'motivated by financial gain to such an extent that they will knowingly fight for an unjust cause'.[19]

As Steinhoff's discussion makes clear, and as Lynch and Walsh also point out,[20] there is no particular reason to think that mercenaries *must* be lucrepaths, or even that they *usually* are. Certainly there is no connection of a logical kind between being a lucrepath on the one hand and, on the other, a person who is 'contracted to provide military services to groups other than his own' and who is 'ready to deliver this service even if this involves taking part in hostilities'. Steinhoff's discussion points out that there is good reason to doubt whether the pecuniary motive is the overriding one for most of those who have been called mercenaries. Indeed it is far more likely that, like the soldier of a national militia, their motives are mixed. An additional point here[21] is that there seems little reason to think that a soldier of a national military could not be a lucrepath (though, admittedly, not an especially successful one), and if this is so, then lucrepathology cannot be a useful way of distinguishing between the moral standing of all mercenaries, on the one hand, and the set of all members of national military forces on the other.

Pattison for one is not moved by such arguments, contending that 'it would be odd if there were no difference in motivation' between the soldier-for-hire and his state counterpart, and that 'we can expect that financial considerations will figure [more] prominently in the decision-making' of the former, while the latter will be more likely to be 'motivated by other considerations, such as national duty'.[22] Without conceding the point, let us for the sake of argument consider the implications if Pattison is right. What if a mercenary 'just is someone who is essentially motivated by money'?[23] Cécile Fabre argues that while we may think lucrepathology to be morally wrong, even if it *is* a defining characteristic of the mercenary (which, as we have seen, is an empirically questionable claim) it does not make the practice of mercenarism itself immoral:

Individuals do all sorts of things out of mostly financial motivations. They often choose a particular line of work, such as banking or consulting, rather than others, such as academia, largely because of the money. They often decide to become doctors rather than nurses for similar reasons. Granting that their interest in making such choices, however condemnable their motivations, is important enough to be protected by a claim (against non-interference) and a power (to enter the relevant employment contracts), it is hard to see how one could deny similar protection to mercenaries.[24]

Another possible justification for the claim that mercenaries are immoral due to the prevalence of an inappropriate motivation is the idea that (contra Machiavelli) mercenaries are *too* bloodthirsty. That is to say, the concern is that mercenaries do what they do out of bloodlust, a psychopathic love of violence and killing. But while that may possibly be true of some contracted combatants, it is doubtful in the extreme that it is true of all of them. Furthermore, this provides no basis on which to distinguish morally between 'mercenaries' on the one hand, and state military personnel on the other. Psychotic killers are just as likely to be drawn to the latter as to the former. In fact, it's arguable that those seeking to satisfy a bloodlust would be more likely to do so within the context of the greater legal protections and opportunities of, say, a state Special Forces unit.

Perhaps then, the question of appropriate motives is not that mercenaries are united by having a particular morally reprehensible motive, but rather that they *lack* a particular motive that is necessary for good moral standing when it comes to fighting and killing. What might such a motive be? Most commentators identify two main candidates, namely 'just cause' and 'right intention', as defined by Just War Theory. As Lynch and Walsh put it, '*Ex hypothesi*, killing in warfare is justifiable only when the soldier in question is motivated amongst other things by a just cause. Justifiable killing motives must not only be non-lucrepathic, but also, following Aquinas, must include just cause and right intention.'[25] But even if we accept, for the sake of argument, that these elements of Just War Theory do apply to individual combatants (a contentious claim which has been the source of much debate among philosophers of war), Lynch and Walsh seem to have a point when they contend it is far from clear that this consideration is one that distinguishes the 'vile mercenary' from the righteous citizen soldier. For it would be bizarre to claim that every member of a national military were so motivated, and equally doubtful that a mercenary could not be motivated in this way when entering into some or all of his contracts. (Historically, we can again think of the case of the Flying Tigers – Chennault himself seems a good example of a 'mercenary' who fought for a just cause and with right intention.) Cécile Fabre makes the interesting point that the fact that the mercenary's obligations stem from individual and specific contracts (rather than the all-encompassing contract between the state warrior and his state) gives him greater control over whether the cause he fights for, and the manner in which he fights, is just. 'On that count, making oneself available for hire on a freelance basis might be less morally risky than joining the army and running the risk of having to obey an unjust order on pain of being dishonourably discharged.'[26]

Even if we presume (again, in defiance of the empirical evidence) that 'mercenaries', by definition, lack the appropriate cause and intention necessary for the just participation in armed hostilities, once again this does not show that the practice of mercenarism is immoral. Here James Pattison points us to a very important distinction, that between intention and motive:

An individual's *intention* is the objective or purpose that they wish to achieve with their action. On the other hand, their *motive* is their underlying reason for acting. It follows that an agent with right intention aims to tackle whatever it is that the war is a just response to, such as a humanitarian crisis, military attack, or serious threat. But their underlying reason for having this intention need not also concern the just cause. It could be, for instance, a self-interested reason.[27]

Thus a 'mercenary' could be motivated entirely by financial gain, yet still have the appropriate intention as a result of his contractual obligations. While we might not think particularly highly of such a person, his actions are not, *per se*, immoral. As Pattison puts it:

> . . . the intrinsic importance of an individual's having a right motive is outweighed by the much higher moral consequences at stake. That is, it pales into insignificance when contrasted with other values that *are* important to the justice or injustice of a war, such as responding to a just cause, using force proportionately, following *jus in bello*, and having a reasonable prospect of success. An individual's mindset seems far less important than these other qualities.[28]

It is also perhaps worth noting that while lucrepathology is certainly a motive to be frowned upon, it is not necessarily the worst motive for someone engaged in armed conflict: As Augustine pointed out, 'The real evils in war are the love of violence, revengeful cruelty, fierce and implacable enmity, wild resistance, and the lust for power.'[29] These evils are all the product of dark *passions*. At the very least the 'pure' lucrepath can be counted upon to be dispassionate.

There is one further version of the 'improper motives' basis for ascribing moral corruption to 'mercenaries' that may yet provide a basis for appropriate moral censure, and here again it is the lack of a motivational element which is important. Here I am referring to the idea that the mercenary is not motivated to fight by a close association with the population on whose behalf he is deploying his military skills, what Lynch and Walsh refer to as 'strong group identification'.[30] The problem with the mercenary, by this interpretation, is that he is a *foreigner*, fighting for a group of people he cannot possibly care deeply about. The corollary to this is that it is a moral principle that one ought only to be willing to fight, kill and possibly die for people with whom one identifies in a close and personal way. But why should this be so? Of course it is not difficult to imagine an argument whereby there exists some sort of moral requirement on us to be willing to fight to defend the social group to which we, in some sense, *belong*, at least where the relevant conditions of a just war are met. But it does not follow from this that there are no *other* circumstances in which a warrior might legitimately practice his deadly trade.

Take the soldiers of many nations who deployed to the Middle East in 1990 and 1991 to eject Saddam Hussein's forces from occupied Kuwait – were they guilty of some serious moral failing? And what of the United Nations' peacekeepers who deploy to and sometimes fight in distant parts of the world, far from their home nations and societies? Quite clearly there are circumstances in which a warrior may ethically be involved in an armed conflict, even where his identification with the group for whose benefit he fights is no more specific than his identification with humanity in general. Furthermore, as we have already seen, there seems no reason to suppose that a mercenary might not, on principle, offer his services only to the group or groups with whom he strongly identifies. Unless this somehow means he is no longer a mercenary, then clearly this consideration is unhelpful in singling out mercenaries for moral condemnation. As Lynch and Walsh put it, 'such considerations are *external* to the practice of mercenarism'.[31]

There is one final possibility that remains to be considered under the 'improper motives' rubric. This is the thought that it is not any one of the above considerations which accounts for the badness of being a 'mercenary', but it is instead the presence of *all* of these motivational factors. So perhaps what matters is holding a very strong (though not lucrepathic) pecuniary motive *plus* not being motivated by such ideals as just cause and right intention *plus* the lack of a strong identification with the group for whom the mercenary is employed to fight. Perhaps, but I don't think so. Firstly, it is hard to see what it is about this combination of these factors that should lead us to a different conclusion to that reached by a consideration of each factor individually. And secondly, it is again not clear that this combination of factors offers sufficient ground to distinguish the mercenary from, say, a South African soldier on African Union peacekeeping duties in the Sudan, who might easily display exactly these characteristics. And finally, it is evident once more that there is nothing about this bundle of characteristics which makes them a necessary feature of being a mercenary – as we have seen above, an individual could quite easily lack all of them yet still fit the definition of a mercenary that I set out earlier in this chapter.

'Mercenary', of course, is not the only derisive term applied to those who exercise warrior skills under commercial contract. Another is 'whores of war'. The assumption here is that an analogy holds between those who contractually provide sexual services and those who contractually provide military services. Both forms of employment vie for the title of the oldest profession, and both are generally considered to be ethically problematic. But just what is it about these 'mercenaries' that supposedly makes them the 'whores of war'?[32] A necessary starting point in assessing this is to consider what it is that is taken to be ethically troublesome about prostitution.

It is worth noting from the start that prostitution is no longer as universally vilified as it once was. Prostitutes are increasingly relabelling themselves as 'sex workers' and demanding recognition as legitimate members of economic society. Arguments in favour of this sort of view tend to be of the liberal contractarian brand advocated by Lars Ericsson, who argues that 'If two adults voluntarily consent to an economic arrangement concerning sexual activity and this activity takes place in private, it seems plainly absurd to maintain that there is something intrinsically wrong with it.'[33] Such arguments are of little interest to us here, of course, for we are in search of reasons why prostitution might be considered to be morally bad.

The response to Ericsson's paper by Carole Pateman sets up nicely one of the dominant lines of argument against prostitution, that which emerges from some quarters of feminism. As Pateman puts it, 'The central feminist argument is that prostitution remains morally undesirable, no matter what reforms are made, because it is one of the most graphic examples of men's domination of women.'[34] Related to this are objections to prostitution on the grounds that it oppresses, endangers or harms the prostitute, or that prostitution results in a violation of one's autonomy.[35] By analogy, then, the objection here, as Fabre puts it, is that 'hiring mercenaries is morally wrong in so far as it consists in treating individuals as little more than both killing machines and cannon fodder'.[36] While this 'objectification objection' is clearly not what we're looking for in seeking out reasons why private warriors themselves might be considered the appropriate targets of moral censure, it's worth mentioning that it is also inadequate as an objection to the privatization of force. As Fabre explains:

> . . . all that the objectification objection does (and that is in fact quite a lot, if off target) is support the view that states have a duty of care to the private soldiers whom they hire – just as they have a duty of care to their armed forces. More specifically, they have a duty to deploy them in accordance with the *jus in bello* requirements of proportionality (whereby the harms done by a particular tactical decision must not exceed the goods it brings about) and necessity (whereby states should risk soldiers' – and civilians' – lives if and only if it would serve their (just) ends).[37]

What we are looking for in trying to discover the moral badness which lies behind the 'whores or war' epithet is some sort of objection to prostitution which would justify the sort of moral censure that lies behind such Old Testament injunctions as the command to burn to death a priest's daughter if she turns to prostitution.[38] What is obvious is that this objection lies within the bounds of the claim that it is not appropriate to offer sex for money. But why is it not appropriate? I have already indirectly dismissed the idea that the problem here is an overriding desire for money (lucrepathology), for though this might well be considered to be morally problematic it is not specific enough to enable us to point the moral finger at the prostitute. So if it is not simply an overriding lust for money which is the problem, it must be that there is something about the nature of sexual relations which makes offering sex on a commercial basis immoral. Here again the Bible is of some help to us, for in it the nation of Israel is often compared to a prostitute when 'she' turns away from the God who has created, chosen, and rescued her.[39] What seems to be at stake here is a particular relationship – prostitution is problematic because it involves a violation or breach of what is deemed to be the appropriate relationship.

Whether this is a legitimate reason for the negative moral judgement on prostitution is not relevant here. The question for us is whether there is a successful analogy between mercenaries and prostitutes, where success is measured by the extent to which one can justify the apportioning of moral censure on mercenaries. Asking this question requires us to heuristically take as given the conservative view of prostitution, regardless of what we actually believe to be true of the morality of prostitution. So then, what is it about commercial soldiering that is supposedly like offering sexual services for pecuniary reward? More specifically, what appropriate relationship is violated or disrupted by the practice of mercenarism? The main candidate in view here is the relationship between citizen and state. Just as it might be argued that the only morally appropriate relationship for the exercise of sexual relations is that between a husband and wife, or between two parties in a committed love relationship, so the implied argument here is that the only morally appropriate relationship for the exercise of martial skills is that between the citizen and the nation of his citizenship. Thus, just as prostitution and other forms of adultery or fornication are seen as violations or disruptions of the morally appropriate sexual relationship, so, by this analogy, mercenarism is a violation or disruption of the morally appropriate martial relationship.

If this is, indeed, the crux of the analogy between the prostitute and the private warrior, then, to state the obvious, the question we must here ponder is whether the relationship between citizen and state is in fact the only appropriate one in the service of which the warfighter can legitimately apply his deadly skills? The relationship between soldier and state is one that I consider in some detail in chapters 4 to 7. But it's enough for now to see that there is a failure of logic implicit in this claim. For while it may well be argued that there is a duty inherent in citizenship that requires the citizen to be prepared to fight for his or her country, it simply does not follow that this means a citizen may *only* fight for his country.[40] What matters instead is that the cause be a just one, and that the fighting be conducted in a morally appropriate manner.

In general, then, it seems we should agree with Lynch and Walsh when they write that:

> . . . many writers . . . base their hostility to mercenarism on a moral analogy with prostitution. But if the strategy is a common one, nonetheless it is inadequate, depending on an extraordinary idealization of appropriate sexual and military relationships, and on a mistaken equation of the morality of intimacy with that of organized violence.[41]

It seems therefore that an investigation into the notion of mercenarism offers little support for the traditional vilification of the character of the soldier-for-hire. The mercenary moniker, then, is an unhelpful one because it offers no unambiguous moral description. I will, therefore dispense with this term for the remainder of this book, and believe that the debate over contracted combatants would benefit from a similar resolution to dispense with this unhelpful label. In the same way the term 'whores of war' turns out to be of little use and should also be set aside. In the next chapter I examine the contracted combatant in the light of the traditional warrior virtues outlined in Chapter 1.

3 The Private Warrior's Virtue

. . . the shift away from the [private] provision of combat services can only be explained by the anti-mercenary norm.

Sarah Percy[1]

We return now to a consideration of the armed private contractor (or contracted combatant or private warrior, as I will also refer to him). In the first chapter we considered the primary virtues which account for the honour in which the state warrior has traditionally been held. In what follows I consider the extent to which these virtues can also be considered appropriate descriptors for private warriors. Referring to the mercenaries of his day, Frederick the Great allegedly described them as displaying 'neither courage, nor loyalty, nor group spirit, nor sacrifice, nor self-reliance'.[2] Should we adopt a similarly jaundiced view of today's contracted combatants?

COURAGE

There is no Medal of Honor nor Victoria Cross for contractors. Whereas the military has a well-developed system by which to recognize acts of courage, there is no parallel system for private warriors. The simple fact is that actions carried out by contracted combatants which would have earned them medals, citations and other forms of recognition if they were in uniformed service, generally go unreported and unnoticed. Among the rare exceptions are a handful of medals and citations awarded by Britain's Royal Humane Society. Instituted in 1774, the Royal Humane Society exists to grant awards 'for acts of bravery in the saving of human life and, also, for the restoration of life by resuscitation'.[3] One recent recipient of the Society's Silver Medal, the oldest and highest honour awarded by the society,[4] is Terry Goodman. According to his citation[5] Goodman, while working for private security firm ArmorGroup, was part of a team guarding a convoy in Basra in 2008. Insurgents attacked the convoy by detonating one or more Improvised Explosive Devices (IEDs) and followed up with heavy small arms and rocket propelled grenade (RPG) fire. Goodman's vehicle was hit by an IED and multiple RPGs, badly injuring him and killing his two crew members. Despite his own wounds he went to the aid of a badly wounded colleague from a different vehicle, saving his colleague's life.

Goodman's case is a straightforward one of extraordinary courage under fire. Examples like these are not as unusual as those suspicious of contracted combatants might think. In April 2004 eight Blackwater contractors, together with a handful of troops from El Salvador and a US Marine, held off a large-scale attack by hundreds of militants on the Coalitions Provisional Authority headquarters in Najaf, Iraq.[6] According to a news report, US spokesman Brig. Gen. Mark Kimmitt described what he saw after the fighting ended as follows:

> 'I stood on a rooftop yesterday in An Najaf, with a small group of American soldiers and coalition soldiers (sic) . . . who had just been through about three and a half hours of combat, I looked in their eyes, there was no crisis. They knew what they were here for,' he continued. 'They'd lost three wounded. We were sitting there among the bullet shells – the bullet casings – and, frankly, the blood of their comrades, and they were absolutely confident.'[7]

In another 2007 incident, in the absence of an immediately available US military response, Blackwater 'Little Bird' helicopters rescued Poland's ambassador to Iraq after his convoy was attacked in an ambush involving militant gunmen and at least three IEDs. The Blackwater helicopter crews intervened despite considerable danger to themselves (at least three people were killed and ten wounded in the attack), and despite having no contractual obligations to do so.[8]

Such actions and many like them which go unreported, give strong testimony to the claim that contractors can, and do, display the warrior virtue of courage. The simple fact is, the decision to take up a contract in a conflict zone as violent as Iraq or Afghanistan have been in recent years itself shows a significant degree of courage. While there has been no shortage of publicity over US and coalition military casualties in these conflicts, contractor casualties have gone largely unnoticed. In a rare exception Reuters special correspondent Bernd Debussmann reported at the beginning of July 2007 that contractor deaths in Iraq and Afghanistan had just breached the 1,000 mark, with a further 13,000 having been wounded. By comparison, US military deaths had by then reached 3,577 meaning that 'on average, since the two conflicts began in 2001 and 2003 respectively, one civilian contractor is killed for every four members of the US Armed Forces'.[9] There's little question that this is a dangerous business, and not one for the faint of heart.

As we saw in the previous chapter, there is also another form of courage which needs to be considered. In addition to the physical courage to face the dangers of combat, the warrior's honour demands also the moral courage to stand firm in the face of illegal orders or peer pressure, and exercise restraint and discernment on the battlefield. The latter form of courage is, in many respects, considerably harder to measure, and obvious examples are hard to come by for the simple reason that this form of courage is usually about *not* acting. This is made all the more difficult because, as J. J. Messner points out, 'in many ways, the industry tends to prefer shunning the spotlight'.[10] But there are nonetheless some telling observations which can be made. For one thing, given the scale of violence in the wars in Afghanistan and Iraq, and the fact that armed contractors and the people and things they guard are a particular target for the insurgents, it is note-worthy that there have been relatively few incidents reported of these contractors not exercising restraint and discernment when facing violent attack. For example ArmorGroup, which in 2006/7 had 1,200 employees in Iraq (over half of them locally contracted Iraqis), estimates that those contractors were attacked by insur-gents over 500 times during that one-year period.[11] A typical attack is described by Norwegian photo-journalist Morten Hvaal, who 'embedded' with an ArmorGroup team in Iraq in late 2006:

> The next day we come under fire. A hundred or so AK-47 rounds hit our convoy. We have been stationary on the highway because of a broken-down truck for more than 20 minutes, in plain view of a small village. More than enough time for insurgents to improvise an attack. We have become a target of opportunity. One of the four armored escort vehicles moves along the convoy on the exposed side, checking for casualties and damage to vehicles. An unarmored truck has several bullet impacts and a badly shaken but unhurt driver. 'Move, move, move! Get them moving,' the team leader urges over the radio. After a few long minutes of hectic improvised repairs, the convoy is again moving towards its destination, a U.S. military base in northern Iraq. None of the 16 heavily-armed security operators in the four armored pickup trucks with gun turrets on the back have fired a shot.[12]

Much has been made of tragic events such as the alleged illegal killings of 17 Iraqi civilians by Blackwater contractors in Baghdad's Nisoor Square on 16 September 2007.[13] But, without in any way condoning the excessive use of armed force, we need to recognize that in a large-scale military operation and under the extreme stresses of combat, it is unrealistic to expect such things will never happen. And it is by no means fair or accurate to view this as a contractor-specific problem. On 4 March 2007 an esti-mated eight to 16 civilians were allegedly killed by US Marines in Shinwar, Afghanistan after their convoy was attacked by a suicide bomber.[14] In a similar set of circumstances on 19 November

2007, another squad of US Marines allegedly killed 24 Iraqi men, women and children in the city of Haditha in retaliation for an IED attack on their convoy.[15]

Events like these alleged killings are tragic and reprehensible, and I offer no apology for combatants who are guilty of the excessive use of force. But the reality that a handful of the many thousands of soldiers and contractors who serve daily under conditions of incredible stress *do* lose control and exceed the bounds of what is legally and morally acceptable, does not for a minute impugn the character of the vast majority who steadfastly and courageously exercise restraint in the face of enormous provocation. In the aftermath of the Nisoor Square events of 16 September 2007, many critics of the private military/security industry claimed this as evidence supporting their view that contracted combatants are not legitimate actors in zones of armed conflict. But, to my knowledge, no such claim was made about the US Marine Corps in response to Shinwar or Haditha. The handful of events so often singled out in the media needs to be weighed against the broader history of the excessive use of force by both contracted and state combatants. As David Isenberg points out, 'even the worst mercenaries from the Middle Ages to the era of decolonization in the mid-twentieth century could not rival the human suffering and physical destruction perpetrated by regular military forces. Mercenaries did not invent concentration camps, firebomb cities from the air, or use nuclear, chemical or biological weapons. In fact, the bloodiest episodes in the 20th century – the bloodiest century in recorded human history – came courtesy of regular military forces.'[16]

COMRADESHIP

Perhaps we might be inclined to accept that contracted combatants can and do display courage. But what about comradeship? Is there some inherent flaw in the character of the contracted combatant, such that he cannot be considered a trustworthy comrade when the chips are down? Certainly there have been well publicized incidents of strained relations between contractors and uniformed personnel. For example, in June 2005 the *Los Angeles Times* reported that Marines deployed in Fallujah had detained 19 members of a North Carolina based company, Zapata Engineering, for three days. The Marines alleged the contractors had fired on Iraqi civilians, while the contractors claimed it was a case of mistaken identity and accused the Marines of verbally and physically abusing them.[17]

Incidents such as these, however, are not in themselves an indication of a problem particular to contractors. The stresses of combat and the fog of war regularly result in tensions between coalition partners involved in military operations. In July 2009, for example, a senior Iraqi Army commander attempted to detain a group of US soldiers after they had responded to an ambush in Baghdad, allegedly for firing indiscriminately at civilians.[18]

It is an old adage that good news is not news. The numerous cases of contractors professionally fulfilling their duties alongside and in partnership with their uniformed or other government colleagues are simply not newsworthy. But cooperation (in, for example, sharing intelligence), while not perfect, is an ongoing and everyday occurrence. Genuine cases of comradeship within the contracted combatant community are numerous, and exemplified by Terry Goodman's heroic action in saving a team-mate's life in Basra in 2008. As we saw, Blackwater contractors, troops from El Salvador, and a US Marine worked together seamlessly in Najaf in 2004.

Another incident involving ArmorGroup contractors is also instructive.[19] On 10 June 2007 US troops manning a well protected checkpoint on a highway overpass six miles east of the city of Mahmoudiya in Iraq came under devastating attack. The insurgents carrying out the attack cunningly detonated a massive Suicide Vehicle-Borne Improvised Explosive Device (SVBIED) under the overpass, collapsing it and bringing the entire checkpoint and its occupants crashing down on the highway below. First on the scene was a passing convoy, under the protection of a team of ArmorGroup security contractors driving armoured Ford F250 SUVs. Despite the very significant danger of a follow-up attack, the ArmorGroup team stopped to assist. Some members of the ArmorGroup team established all-round defence of the site, while others grabbed medical kits and went to the assistance of the wounded soldiers lying in the rubble. Once US military help arrived, the contractors continued working alongside the quick reaction force for 45 minutes to stabilize the situation, before continuing along the road with their convoy once they deemed they had done all they could.

As J. J. Messner points out, 'the ArmorGroup contract did not include a clause that required their employees to save people from disaster. There was no contractual obligation requiring these employees to do what they did. Regardless, these contractors put their own safety on the line and provided assistance where it was needed, with no thought to anything other than the lives of the trapped survivors.'[20] Three soldiers died that day, but matters would certainly have been worse had the ArmorGroup contractors not displayed the warrior virtue of comradeship on that occasion. Sadly, only days later one of the contractors involved was himself killed by insurgents.[21] There can be little question he and his colleagues displayed the warrior virtue of comradeship.

SENSE OF HONOUR

Joseph Runzo, Professor of Philosophy and Religious Studies at Chapman University, has argued[22] that the private warrior lacks the critical quality of honour (by which term he seems to mean an appropriate sense of honour), which disqualifies him from being ethically employed in combat. Runzo's argument is perhaps unique in focusing on this particular virtue, and is therefore worth considering in some detail.

Firstly, Runzo is troubled by the thought that 'the personnel of a private military company neither systematically studies military law and Just War Theory nor operates under the purview of military law.'[23] While this may well have been true in the past, it is clearly not an *intrinsic* problem with the private warrior. Indeed, since October 2007 battlefield contractors under contract to the US government have been coming to terms with the implications of new legislation that brings them under the Uniform Code of Military Justice of the US armed forces.[24] One wonders also to what extent it is true that private warriors lack the necessary grasp of military law and Just War Theory. Given that private military companies tend to mostly employ personnel with military backgrounds, it seems likely there is a fair degree of proficiency in these matters among private warriors. Added to this is the fact that the industry is increasingly taking self-regulatory steps to ensure its members act ethically on the battlefield. For example IPOA, one of the largest associations of private military and security companies, has run training programmes aimed at 'field managers and independent contractors' which have the goal of serving

> . . . as a mechanism by which the IPOA Code of Conduct and other standards can be operationalized by contractors active in conflict and post-conflict environments around the world. Participants will be trained in essential areas such as international humanitarian law, NGO/IO interaction, cultural, gender and religious sensitivities and learn how to operationalize field guidelines, increase productivity levels and to improve interaction with other actors.[25]

The second problem with PMCs which concerns Runzo is that, while they may provide some short-term military advantage, they are not suited to the long-term endeavour of building peace, because 'they are not in the business of reconciliation'.[26] Herfried Münkler argues the same point when he writes that, although private warriors might be of value for some tasks, 'It is quite another question whether this kind of soldier is the best suited for

operations designed to end a war and to bring peace; "freelanc-
ers" can scarcely be expected to have the discipline and incorruptibility that are an essential condition for the success of such
operations.'[27] As is common in discussions of private warriors, this
sweeping statement draws in a range of issues and includes no
actual argument (beyond appealing to widely held prejudices)
to support its conclusion. So let us attempt to untangle it. We can
set aside the issues of discipline and 'incorruptibility' (by which I
take it Münkler means something like moral courage), as we have
addressed these above. What is left is an unexplained and unsup-
ported assumption that private warriors are not 'in the business'
of achieving peace and reconciliation.

But why not, exactly? It's perhaps worth pointing out that the
leading trade organization for the private military/security industry is IPOA, which has the motto 'Businesses Worldwide. United
for *Peace*' (italics added). Anyone who takes the time to visit the
websites of companies who provide armed security services in
conflict zones will see most if not all of them see themselves as 'in
the business' of securing peace (or at least the business mitigat-
ing risk). Of course, opponents of the industry will dismiss this
as Orwellian propaganda. Certainly it is not uncommon to hear
it argued that, because these companies make their money in
conflict zones it is in their interests to extend rather than resolve
conflicts – as if there were some shortage of conflicts in the
world for these companies to address! But all this misses a critical
point for, in Runzo's analysis at least, there has been a category
error in ascribing to individual private warriors a lack of honour
because of characteristics allegedly found in the companies that
employ them. I address this issue with regard to the companies
in chapters 6 and 7 of this book, when I deal with what I call civil–
(private) military relations and the issue of 'shirking'. But what of
the individual private warrior? Why, exactly, should we think him
'unsuited' to the task of building peace?

A key point to consider here once again is that the typical
private warrior is a former state military soldier, marine, sailor

or airman. There have certainly been concerns expressed about the suitability of military personnel to the task of building peace. As the old – and arguably increasingly outdated – saying goes, the job of the military is to 'kill people and break things'. But the private warrior's former military service can hardly be considered to make him less suited to the task of ending conflict than his counterpart still in uniform! The assumption here seems generally to go in the opposite direction – the private warrior, while once a respectable and respected member of his nation's military, has, by dint of signing a commercial contract requiring him to make use of the skills learned while in the military, suddenly developed a sleazy and untrustworthy character. Of course the assumption is never put this baldly, because so described its unsustainability is obvious.

It should be kept in mind, as mentioned in the previous chapter, that the trend by most Western militaries to move from conscription based forces to all-volunteer forces (AVF) gave rise to concerns that the traditional warrior's sense of honour would become degraded. There is, however, no evidence that this has taken place. Given that the private warrior is, in a sense, the ultimate volunteer (signing up as he does for individual missions), is there any particular reason to think this particular trend will erode the all-important sense of honour? Certainly I have yet to hear a convincing reason why this should be the case. If it turns out to be true that, as Robinson suggests, '[t]he concern for external validation may even be hardwired into human biology',[28] then there is even less reason to think such an erosion is likely to happen.

Given the lack of any real reason to think the private warrior must intrinsically lack the honour of his uniformed counterpart, we can set this particular objection aside. But it does raise an important question. If, as I am arguing in this book, there turns out to be no reason to hold the private warrior who adheres to the spirit and principles of the just conduct of war to be unethical, then is there not a duty by the nation who benefits from his services to honour him appropriately? We think it a moral failing when a nation does not appropriately honour its men and women in the military, or those who serve in the nation's police forces, or its firefighters. It's hard to see why a different standard should be deemed to apply for those who take on significant risks in contributing to stabilization efforts in the world's conflict zones.

PROFESSIONALISM

Among philosophers who address the ethical challenges of armed conflict, one name stands out: Michael Walzer. His 1977 book *Just and Unjust Wars* is a modern classic, and the measure against which similar works are held to account. In an article published in *The New Republic* in March 2008, Walzer turned his attention to private contractors.[29] His article seems to have been partially stimulated by the publication of Jeremy Scahill's *Blackwater: The Rise of the World's Most Powerful Mercenary Army*. While generally positively disposed towards Scahill's book, Walzer is nonetheless critical of Scahill's failure 'actually to make the argument against mercenaries – and not merely to assume it'. Walzer therefore takes it on himself to sketch out the central lines of that moral argument.

At the heart of Walzer's argument is an analogy he draws between Iraq's private militias and American security contracting firms like Blackwater. While admitting that firms like Blackwater are not fighting a private war ('Iraq is an American war', he concedes), Walzer nonetheless persists in treating security contracting firms as if they were private armies controlled by warlords. While he doesn't express it in exactly these terms, his comparison betrays a concern relevant to our analysis here, namely the worry that armed private contractors and the firms that employ them do not fit under the rubric of 'professional military forces'. As we saw in Chapter 1, a key defining feature of the military professional is his politically neutral service to the state. Private militias, on the other hand, are in no way neutral, nor do they serve the state (except, perhaps, when doing so fulfils some narrow sectarian or other such interest). Another way of putting the difference is that military professionals can be properly trusted with the security of the nation they serve, while militias cannot.

But why think of contracted combatants in this way? The private security contractors active in Iraq are all on contract to, or operating with the consent of, the US and Iraqi governments. Walzer is entirely correct to point out that, following Max Weber's definition, the state is both constituted and justified by its monopoly on the use of force. But he makes a glaring error in thinking it is only through the military that the state may exercise its monopoly.

As Duke University's Professor Peter Feaver reminds us in his important recent treatment of democratic civil–military relations,[30] the different branches of the military are *not* themselves the state, but are rather the 'armed servants' of the state. This is precisely why the notion of civil–military relations exists – it articulates the challenge of ensuring obedience by the armed agents of the state to the state's democratically elected principals.

An elected government may consent to a private entity employing armed force on its behalf in two ways: either directly through contracting it, or indirectly, by consenting to its employment to provide security to another private individual or enterprise. In both cases the entity concerned becomes, like the branches of the military and other security forces, an agent of the state. Of course the state may not directly oversee each and every activity undertaken by those agents (Walzer seems particularly bothered by the thought that security contractors in Iraq 'get into fire-fights on their own, for their own reasons'). But if this in itself undermines the state's monopoly on force, then so do the activities of the rent-a-cop at your local shopping mall. True, rent-a-cops are not employees of the state, but they are nonetheless agents of the state in the sense that they contribute to the enforcement of the state's monopoly on force by helping to enforce the law.

The key issue, as I will argue in Chapter 7, is control. Control can be achieved through direct oversight by the elected government or, more commonly, by the elected principals granting a mandate and setting up constraints (the rent-a-cop falls into the latter category). Walzer is no doubt right that there has been inadequate state (whether US or Iraqi) control over contractors in Iraq. But this should not come as a surprise, nor should it be cause for alarm. The degree of contractor support for operations in Iraq is, as is regularly noted, unprecedented. It's therefore no surprise that the governments involved are still struggling with how to ensure control over them. But this does not suggest (as Walzer's article seems to me to imply) that a lack of state control is some intrinsic flaw in the nature of private security contracting, or even that the practical difficulties make this an insurmountable issue. If states can manage to hold military personnel accountable for their actions in far flung and chaotic environments, then there's no reason in principle why the same cannot apply to their other (contracted) agents.

The question of appropriate control is one of the most important and widely misunderstood issues relevant to the ethics of the outsourcing of military force. So important is it that it is, from various angles, the focal point of the next four chapters. For now I hope this brief discussion is sufficient to induce the reader to temporarily suspend scepticism on this front.

But of course professionalism is not simply about trustworthiness and control. As previously noted, it also involves possessing and continuing to expand the core expertise of the military profession. In addition, the military professional both identifies with, and is identified by society as a member of, the military profession. Do, or can, private contractors fulfil these criteria?

Doubtless these contractors generally *possess* the necessary expertise – they are hired on the basis of their previous military service. One of the common complaints about the private military/security industry is that it has created too strong a demand for those with military skills, with the result that military units, and elite units in particular, are having trouble retaining valuable skilled personnel. It is somewhat contradictory for those opposed to the outsourcing of military force to complain about this, while claiming that those very same contractors are unprofessional and untrustworthy.

In considering the question of whether contractors contribute to increasing the core expertise of the military profession, we find ourselves expanding the scope of our enquiry from just 'boots on the ground' contractors to include those who offer military analysis, advice and training. This is, of course, one of the core business areas of the industry, and the bread and butter of firms like MPRI and DynCorp. Thus it's not unreasonable to claim that private contractors not only *do* contribute to the core expertise of the military profession, but in fact have also become increasingly indispensable to this endeavour.

The final issue concerning professionalism is whether or not the contracted combatant qualifies as a professional through his identification with the military profession and, perhaps more importantly, society's recognition of him as a military professional. This question of societal recognition or 'legitimacy' is a vital one, so much so that in a sense it overshadows everything else addressed in this book. As a consequence, I shall refrain from addressing this issue directly until the book's conclusion. For now it is enough to note Andrew Abbott's wise observation that a profession's legitimacy is not a fixed and immutable fact of nature.[31] As Cook puts it, 'society may confer legitimacy on a profession or remove it'.[32]

SACRIFICE

The astute reader will have noticed I have departed from the structure of Chapter 1 by leaving the issue of sacrifice until last. This is because it is on the issue of sacrifice where we see the first real moral difference between the armed contractor and the soldier, sailor, marine or airman of a national military force, and so needs to be singled out. As we have seen, it is a critical element of the state warrior's virtue that he be willing to sacrifice his life or physical well-being in service of his country. The same simply cannot be said of the armed contractor. To concede this is not for a moment to suggest that individual contractors cannot display great courage (as we saw above) or make heroic sacrifices.[33] The point is rather that this cannot be *required* or *expected* of the contractor. There are circumstances in which military commanders can, and should, send or lead his troops on missions where there is a significant likelihood that successfully completing those missions will require the death or injury of some, many, or even all of those under his command. This is because built into the idea of national military service there is a presumption that what would be supererogatory for the average citizen – the willingness to give up life and limb – is, under appropriate circumstances, normative for military personnel. The same is certainly not true for the contracted combatant. While individuals who join private military companies accept a significantly higher level of risk in their field of employment than in most other occupations, this simply does not equate to a requirement that they be willing to sacrifice themselves for some higher good. Sacrifice has no place in the cost-benefit analysis at the heart of commercial soldiering.

What is clear from this is that while there is a significant range of operations in which armed contractors and military personnel can be viewed as on a moral par, there is also a range of operations, those which may meaningfully demand sacrifice, for which it would be morally inappropriate to deploy private forces. There is, however, a flip side to this. As I will argue in the final chapter of this book, there is a case to be made that the contractual and episodic nature of the contracted combatant's service makes him morally more suited than his uniformed counterpart for a different range of missions, such as humanitarian interventions.

On this issue of sacrifice, then, the virtues which can be expected of the private warrior differ from those of his uniformed counterpart. But this should neither surprise nor dismay us. For it is nobody's contention that private forces should perform precisely the same role as national military forces, or that contracted combatants should replace uniformed state military forces. And the difference here described does not result in *dishonour* for the private warrior. Instead it points to a difference in which roles he should be employed.

CONCLUSION

The goal of this and the preceding chapter has been to evaluate the private warrior's virtue. I have presented an analysis of the question of whether the private warrior suffers from some intrinsic character flaw for which he deserves dishonour, and which makes him morally unsuited to the task of conducting just military operations. I began, in the previous chapter, by examining the derogatory terms 'mercenary' and 'whores of whore' which are often applied to the private warrior, and concluded that these terms are without meaningful descriptive content. I then turned to an assessment of the applicability of the traditional warrior virtues to the private warrior. It became clear, on consideration, that there are no intrinsic flaws which apply generally to the character of private warriors such that they are unable to display courage, exhibit comradeship and a sense of discipline, or lack an appropriate sense of honour. Indeed there is compelling evidence of private warriors showing all of these characteristics.

This should not come as a surprise. Most armed contractors are former military or law enforcement personnel. Why should we expect, as Messner puts it, that on becoming contractors some universal condition applies which has the consequence that these individuals 'leave their morals, ethics, honor and sense of duty at the door'?[34] Consider, by way of example, Art Laguna, a Blackwater contractor who was killed in January 2007 when the 'Little Bird' helicopter he was piloting was shot down after responding to a call for assistance from a US Embassy convoy that came under attack in downtown Baghdad.[35] Laguna was a three-decade veteran of the US Army and National Guard who served three tours in Iraq and one in Bosnia. At home he served as a sheriff's reserve deputy. He was posthumously awarded the Legion of Merit by the US military for 'exceptional conduct in the performance of outstanding services and achievements', and had previously been awarded a medal by the California Department of Corrections 'for piloting a National Guard helicopter that helped save a California man who'd been stranded by floodwaters on the roof of his car'.[36] Is there any fundamental reason why we should doubt Mr Laguna's wife's assertion that 'Art considered his job with the private security firm that protects US diplomats in Iraq a continuation of his service to this country'?[37] What of her claim that this father of four and grandfather of six was a hero and a man of honour?

Of course there are contractors who lack courage, honour and professionalism. But this is also true of some soldiers, airmen, sailors and marines. In fact, in all likelihood those contracted combatants of dubious morals were once also uniformed combatants of dubious morals. But this in no way shows there is something intrinsically questionable about the character of contracted combatants in general.

The final focal point of the chapter was on the question of sacrifice. While acknowledging that willingness to sacrifice life and limb in the service of a particular nation is not a virtue that can be expected of the private warrior, the difference in roles between private warriors and their state counterparts means this does not lead to dishonour for the private warrior, and indeed (as we shall see) there are important tasks the private warrior may legitimately take on for which he is arguably morally better suited than the state warrior.

All of this is, of course, important, for if there were some fundamental lack of virtue inherent in the private warrior then it would clearly be problematic to employ his services, though even Walzer contends that dire circumstances might suffice to warrant the employment of the dreaded 'mercenary'.[38] Walzer's comment makes it clear that the individual private warrior's virtue is only part of the question. There are also consequentialist considerations to be taken into account. Walzer believes good consequences can, in extreme circumstances, outweigh bad virtue in the actors that bring them about. The question I consider in the remainder of this book is similar, but inverted. Given the private warrior's virtue, are there nonetheless consequentialist concerns which should make us question the morality of making use of the private warrior's services?

4   The Right to Fight

The right to use physical force is ascribed to other institutions or individuals only to the extent that the state permits it. The state is considered the sole source of the 'right' to use violence.

Max Weber[1]

What, exactly, are states *for*? Perhaps the most famous answer to that question was given in the mid-seventeenth century by the political philosopher Thomas Hobbes. In his classical work *Leviathan*, among the most influential treatises on political philosophy ever written, Hobbes asks his reader to consider what life would be like in a world where there is no political authority. In this hypothetical 'state of nature', Hobbes argued, all of us would be in a perpetual state of war against one another, and life would be 'solitary, poor, nasty, brutish, and short'. To escape the state of nature, rationally self-interested individuals will enter into a 'social contract' with one another. This contract has two fundamental aspects. Firstly, all those who enter into this contract agree to create a society by refraining to exercise such rights as the right to defend their lives and property with force. Secondly, and as a consequence, all must agree to live under the authority of a sovereign who will enact and enforce laws to ensure the harmony of society. This is what gives the state its monopoly over the legitimate use of force, which sociologist Max Weber famously asserted in his landmark 1918 speech *Politik als Beruf* is the central defining characteristic of the modern state.[2] Patricia Owens describes the emergence of this norm as follows:

> Since the seventeenth century, the public realm in European nation-states has been associated with governmental administration of the commonwealth. The state monopolized the right to declare itself as the primary 'public' arena through its claim to successfully represent and defend the general interests of those it governed. The modern state form showed itself to be the most efficient and well-equipped entity for offering a way to achieve the 'first freedom' as it is understood in most western political thought – 'security-from-violence'. The Leviathan removed the individual and groups of individuals from the state of nature. Since Hobbes, the protection and fostering of life have been understood as the liberal solution to the problem of persuading individuals to submit to the Leviathan. In giving up unfettered liberty, citizens have the right to expect certain benefits and rewards. In exchange for obedience to the sovereign's process of power accumulation, the state provides a way of life in which the pursuit of 'private' interests is made compatible with the 'public' good. The 'public' is synonymous with 'government' and its primary rationale is the sustenance of life.[3]

Social contract theory, as articulated in its many forms by philosophers like Hobbes, John Locke,[4] Jean-Jacques Rousseau and John Rawls, is without question the most influential political theory to address the nation state. And while there are many variants of the theory, all agree that the most fundamental justification for the state's existence is its role in providing safety and security to those living within its territory. As Cécile Fabre puts it 'the state's right to wage war is one which it has precisely in so far as it is better than individuals at protecting their fundamental human rights through the use of lethal force'.[5] Indeed, it is exceedingly rare to come across a modern political theorist of any stripe who would disagree with this claim. This is what gives the state's use of force in defence of its citizens the positive moral standing which is expressed in Just War Theory and international law. But it has not always been this way. Before the nation state arose, and with it the idea of the state's moral responsibility to its citizens, Augustine expressed a somewhat more jaundiced view of the kingdoms of his day:

> Remove justice, and what are kingdoms but gangs of criminals on a large scale? What are criminal gangs but petty kingdoms? A gang is a group of men under the command of a leader, bound by a compact of association in which plunder is divided according to an agreed convention. If this villainy wins so many recruits from the ranks of the demoralized that it acquired territory, establishes a base, captures cities and subdues peoples, it then openly arrogates to itself the title of kingdom, which is conferred on it in the eyes of the world, not by the renouncing of aggression but by the attainment of impunity. For it was a witty and truthful rejoinder which was given by a captured pirate to Alexander the Great. The king asked the fellow, 'What is your idea, in infesting the sea?' And the pirate answered 'The same as yours, in infesting the earth! But because I do it with a tiny craft, I'm called a pirate: because you have a mighty navy, you're called an emperor.'[6]

The fact that most contemporary readers will find Augustine's view expressed here excessively cynical is due in large part to the enormous influence that social contract theory, and political liberalism more broadly, has had on our thinking and on the nature of the nation state. As military ethicist Martin Cook reminds us, 'it is important in our thinking about fighting in *defense of states* to remind ourselves that the state as we know it is a fairly modern invention'.[7] As Cook further points out, 'It is an axiom of this new model of international order that all states *have equal moral claims* to territorial integrity and political sovereignty, and that *each state* has the right to be free of aggression by others and to use its military in defense of those rights.'[8]

The right to 'national-defence' might well be axiomatic in today's international order, but the normative basis of this 'right' is not as straightforward as it might at first seem. In his book *War and Self-Defense*, Oxford University philosopher David Rodin contends that the seemingly unassailable position of national-defence is unjustified, at least as this notion is understood in contemporary Just War Theory and international law. In his book Rodin considers what he argues are the two main justifications for national-defence. Both, he maintains, lean heavily on the moral legitimacy of self-defence. The first does so by means of a reductive argument – the idea that national-defence is, in effect, the 'collective form' of self-defence. This can be understood either as the claim that national-defence is 'simply an application, *en masse*, of the familiar right of individuals to protect themselves and others from unjust lethal attack',[9] or as the claim that 'the state has an obligation (and therefore a right) to defend its citizens in much the same way a parent has the right to defend his or her child'.[10] The second justification for national defence which Rodin addresses is what he calls the 'analogical strategy', which is most famously articulated as Michael Walzer's 'domestic analogy' in which 'the rights and duties of states can be understood on the model of the rights and duties of individual persons'.[11] After giving close attention to both of these approaches to justifying national-defence, Rodin concludes that 'National-defense cannot be reduced to a collective application of personal rights of self-defense, and it cannot be explained as a state-held right analogous to personal self-defense. Because the right of national-defense has always been the central "just cause" for war within the Just War Theory, and because the analogy with self-defense has always been its central justification, this result must be seen as a serious challenge to the traditional Just War doctrine of international morality.'[12]

In this book I am considering the moral status of contracted combatants when compared to that of their uniformed counterparts. Is there, or could there be, a group of contracted combatants who live up to the moniker of 'Just Warriors, Inc.'? Answering this presupposes there is such a thing as a just warrior in the first place. If Rodin is right, and national-defence lacks an appropriate normative basis, then it is doubtful whether there are any meaningful circumstances in the world we actually live in[13] which would allow a warrior to justly employ force. But this is so strongly counter-intuitive that Rodin's conclusion must be resisted. In this chapter I explore the central features of Rodin's critique and offer a brief account of the state's 'right to fight', which I argue is normatively valid. I then return to the main theme of the book, and consider how the employment of contracted combatants fares in the light of the account I develop.

NATIONAL-DEFENCE AND THE COMMON LIFE

David Rodin's goal is to establish whether or not there exists a successful account of the right to national-defence which is 'substantially co-extensive with the way that right is understood in modern international law and the best interpretation of the Just War Theory'.[14] In particular, he argues, such an account must establish a right to national-defence which is held by all sovereign states, regardless of their particular forms of government. As I have said, the second approach to justifying national-defence (after the reductive strategy) which Rodin considers is what he calls the 'analogical strategy', an approach which attempts to establish a right of national-defence that is analogous to the personal right of self-defence. Because the argument I develop in the next section falls broadly into this category, I will focus only on Rodin's arguments relevant to this broad strategy.

The idea of 'the common life' is central to this approach, in which 'national-defense is a right held by states and grounded principally in the end, not of defending the lives of individual citizens, but of defending the common life of the community'.[15] Rodin identifies four interpretations of the common life as a potential justification for national-defence, though he rejects one outright and concentrates his attention on the remaining three. The rejected interpretation comes to light in one reading of the work of Hegel, namely the view that 'the common life is a source of value independent of its value for individual persons'[16] in which the rights and value of individuals are derived from the community to which they belong. Put another way, the claim here is that the value inherent in the community itself stands independent of, and prior to, the value that community might have for individual persons. Rodin rejects this view on the grounds that moral explanations, if they are to carry any weight, must derive their legitimacy from their contribution to individual human life.

The three remaining interpretations of the common life are given closer attention. Firstly, there is the approach which is rooted directly in Hobbesean social contract theory and which is based on the legitimacy of a state which arises out of its ability to provide order in the affairs of its citizens, who thereby escape the inconveniences of the state of nature. Rodin responds that this cannot provide grounds for a right to national-defence against aggressors whose goal is to substitute their own rule for the order provided by the home state. What is needed, he points out, is 'a moral reason not simply to defend order, but to defend a particular form of order; to defend *our* order'.[17]

This leads Rodin to consider the second approach to grounding national-defence in the common life. This approach recognizes that our identity is in some sense partially defined by the particular cultural and linguistic background provided by our community, and that we locate our lives within the history of that community. These are things we recognize as goods of the first order, and supporters of this approach therefore claim that the particular character of the common life can properly function as the end of the right of national-defence, for the state's role is to protect and foster the unique character of the common life, as well as to embed the values and commitments of the community in its structures.

The main problem here, according to Rodin, is that such a view fails to achieve the level of objectivity required to support a universal right of national-defence. The value of any particular form of common life is evident only to those within that common life, not to those beyond it: 'it is not apparent why someone who is not a participant in that particular common life should recognize its distinctive form as a good and a value'.[18] Rodin points out, further, that states which show a clear disregard for human rights, but which fall below the currently accepted threshold for humanitarian intervention (a disregard which, we may assume, runs contrary to the common life of the people in those states), are nonetheless clearly possessors of the right of national-defence in international law and under most interpretations of Just War Theory. One attempt at getting around this problem of the subjectivity of the common life is through a relativization of value in which it is impossible for us to judge the value of a mode of life which is not ours. This approach functions by claiming that value relativism means we cannot legitimately judge across boundaries and therefore must abstain from intervening in other communities. This, therefore (it is argued), gives rise to a right to national-defence which is the flip side of this duty of non-interference. But this approach, Rodin argues, requires accepting a relativism of value in all cases except for the case of non-intervention, which must be objectively valuable in order for the argument to succeed. Rodin dismisses this as hopelessly ad hoc.

This failure of the 'subjective' view brings into focus the final interpretation of a common life-based right of national-defence. In this approach what is needed is 'a value that is both objective and particular – it must be objective and recognizable as valid across cultures, yet still provide a reason for defending a particular state or community'.[19] Freedom, autonomy and particularly self-determination seem to some thinkers, most notably Michael Walzer, to fit the bill here. These seem to be objectively valued goods which underpin all particular notions of the common good. Furthermore, the argument continues, these goods can only be protected if state sovereignty is respected, and so from this a universal right to national-defence arises.

The obvious objection here, as Rodin rightly recognizes, is that only democratic societies truly provide the opportunity for self-determination, so this sort of argument could only apply to democratic states. But this, of course, is insufficient to the task of finding a basis for the near-universal possession by states of the right to national defence. Michael Walzer attempts to avoid this by arguing that in all states there is a process of 'working out' what form of political regime is in place, and that this process is one of collective self-determination. Rodin contends, however, that this is a case of stretching the notion of self-determination beyond all recognition, and concludes, therefore, that this final view is also an inadequate justification for the right of national-defence. Thus he concludes that, despite our strong intuitions to the contrary, national-defence as it is understood in contemporary Just War Theory and in international law cannot be a justification for resorting to war.

BEYOND THE PRIMACY OF RIGHTS THESIS

In this section I set out an alternative account of the common life as a potential end of national-defence, one not considered by Rodin because, I will argue, of an implicit commitment to what the renowned Canadian philosopher Charles Taylor calls the 'primacy of rights thesis'. It seems to me that this alternative offers the potential to avoid the sceptical conclusion Rodin reaches.

Taylor describes the primacy of rights thesis as follows:

Theories which assert the primacy of rights are those which take as the fundamental, or at least a fundamental, principle of their political theory the ascription of certain rights to individuals, and which deny the same status to a principle of belonging or obligation, that is a principle which states our obligation as men (*sic*) to belong to or sustain society, or a society of a certain type, or to obey authority or an authority of a certain type. Primacy-of-right theories in other words accept a principle ascribing rights to men as binding unconditionally, binding, that is, on men as such. But they do not accept as similarly unconditional a principle of belonging or obligation. Rather our obligation to belong to or sustain a society, or to obey its authorities, is seen as derivative, as laid on us conditionally, through our consent, or through its being to our advantage.[20]

This primacy of rights thesis rests on a view of human selfhood which conceives of the individual as fundamentally self-sufficient, a view Taylor refers to as 'atomism'. It is easy to see why Taylor links atomism with social contract theory – such an approach is assumed by the very idea of humans existing as independent agents in a state of nature, from which they escape by way of voluntary contract. Against this view, Taylor argues in favour of a range of theories which posit humans as fundamentally social beings:

> The claim is that living in society is a necessary condition of the development of rationality, in some sense of this property, or of becoming a moral agent in the full sense of the term, or of becoming a fully responsible, autonomous being. These variations and other similar ones represent the different forms in which a thesis about man as a social animal have been or could be couched. What they have in common is the view that outside society, or in some variants outside certain kinds of society, our distinctively human capacities could not develop.[21]

Following this approach, rights cannot stand independently of an essential conceptual background which defines the specific forms of human flourishing those rights are intended to protect. Taylor's own view is that our specifically human potential requires not the mere existence of *any* society but rather the existence of specific kinds of society – he is explicit, for example, in his belief that authoritarian societies hinder the development of our distinctly human capacities. There are, Taylor thinks, particular non-contingent features of the human self which can be developed or denied. Such development depends crucially on societal institutions:

... the free individual or autonomous moral agent can only achieve
and maintain his identity in a certain type of culture [which incorpo-
rates certain facets and activities]. But these and others of the same
significance do not come into existence spontaneously each suc-
cessive instant. They are carried on in institutions and associations
which require stability and continuity and frequently also support
from society as a whole – almost always the moral support of being
commonly recognized as important, but frequently also considerable material support. These bearers of our culture include museums,
symphony orchestras, universities, laboratories, political parties, law
courts, representative assemblies, newspapers, publishing houses, tel-
evision stations, and so on. And I have to mention also the mundane
elements of infrastructure without which we could not carry out these
higher activities: buildings, railroads, sewage plants, power grids, and
so on. Thus [the] requirement of a living and varied culture is also the
requirement of a complex and integrated society, which is willing and
able to support all these institutions.[22]

For our purposes, then, this approach can be sketched as
follows. At its foundation is the claim that there are specific
and non-contingent features of the identity of humans which
are essential to true humanness. These features are not always
already there, but rather can and must be developed and
worked out. But this process can only take place within a social
context. Full-blown human development is therefore dependent on the existence of a specific range of societies (for not all
societies will be conducive to the development of the relevant
features of humanness), which in turn will usually require the
existence and support of specific kinds of institutions such as (or
paradigmatically) states (for not all regimes will be conducive
to the support of the relevant sorts of societies). On this view
humans will often be dependent on institutions such as states
for both *attaining* and *maintaining* their fundamental humanness. Because of their fundamental nature, the attributes of full
humanness can legitimately be defended with lethal force under

the right of (individual) self-defence. Furthermore, the right to defend the attributes of full humanness extends to the right to defend the necessary conditions for human flourishing.[23] Thus, because the existence of a state (or equivalent institution) is a necessary condition for the achievement and maintenance of the attributes of full humanness, persons have the right to defend their state (or equivalent institution) with lethal force. On the other hand, states which fail to adequately nurture, or which actively undermine, the conditions necessary for their citizens to achieve true humanness, have no such right to national-defence. Furthermore, it may well be argued that other nations (or the international community) have a duty to intervene in a proportionally appropriate way to ensure those conditions are set in place.

This is, of course, only a sketch. As I give a fuller account of this approach and its resilience in the face of Rodin's concerns elsewhere,[24] I think enough has been said here to show that something like the view I have articulated here provides an account of what is fundamentally human, and shows the dependence of the individual's basic flourishing on the existence of a certain community. Though such communities have obviously not always depended on the existence of modern states, it is equally obvious that in most cases today such dependence does exist. This therefore provides both a general justification, derived from the individual's right to self-defence, for states to use armed force in self-defence, as well as a specific justification for particular states to defend themselves even when an invading state intends to put in place some form of social order (a specificity which is lacking from the standard Hobbesian defence of the right of states to defend themselves – something that Rodin shows to be problematic).

What this approach manifestly does not do is satisfy the requirement that the state *qua* state has an inalienable right to national-defence. As such, it falls foul of Rodin's requirements for a successful account of the right to national-defence. But we should, I think, respectfully disagree with Rodin in this regard. In place of this requirement I argue that, as a matter of principle, every state must be considered to have the *prima facie* right to national-defence, but under certain conditions it may be justifiably concluded that a particular state does not, in fact, have this right.

It seems to me that the emerging doctrine of humanitarian intervention is important here. Rodin himself recognizes this emerging doctrine, or at least its potential emergence, which 'permit[s] intervention in states that engage in widespread violations of human rights against their own citizens'. He however goes on to dismiss this doctrine as irrelevant to the question in hand, on the grounds of its severely limited nature – involving only 'abuses of human rights which are so severe that they "shock the conscience of mankind", typically involving genocide, mass expulsion, or starvation'.[25] This, however, strikes me as an irrelevant consideration. The fact that humanitarian interventions are only justified in particularly extreme situations seems to me to be simply a consequence of the doctrine of proportionality – a recognition that often a military intervention will result in greater hardship than the original offence it aimed to rectify. Like self-defence, humanitarian intervention by means of military force is only one of a range of possible interventions which may be justified in proportion to the appropriateness of their deployment. And of course we *do* feel that nations are justified in intervening in all sorts of ways in response to deeply held views of the nature of human development. Take for example the positive intervention of pouring funds for the education of women into a country where this is not something that has generally been valued.

I will argue in Chapter 8 that the notion of humanitarian intervention, particularly as reflected in the 'responsibility to protect' the norm, has emerged as a legitimate dimension of the ethics of the use of armed force, a revision which is entirely compatible with the theory of national-defence I have outlined here. True, the emerging ethical framework may not correspond to the way Just War Theory was conceived of in, say, Anscombe's classic 1939 piece on the topic,[26] but as Rodin himself says it is rather difficult to establish exactly what Just War Theory *is*, and 'it is more accurate to talk of the "just war tradition" . . . for it includes a large number of diverse yet related positions'.[27] Rodin sees the formulation of Just War Theory as it exists in international law as definitive. But international law is no monolith, and so the changes that are leading to a doctrine of humanitarian intervention must, following this approach, be considered to be changes to the accepted view of Just War Theory. One might even argue that this change is in some sense a partial return to an earlier formulation of Just War Theory. As James Turner Johnson points out, the classical Just War tradition included among the accepted reasons for going to war the just cause of 'the punishment of evil'.[28] While it is unlikely this particular formulation would find too much favour in contemporary discourse, there seems nonetheless to be a significant dose of this in contemporary humanitarian interventions, which are at the very least aimed at preventing further evils and often also bringing to justice those who have perpetrated evil. Accordingly, it seems eminently arguable that the view I have outlined here must, at the very least, be on the cusp of correspondence with the accepted view of Just War Theory.

In conclusion, then, it seems that a doctrine of national-defencse based in the protection of the common life, described in the way I have sketched here, does indeed offer real potential for providing a valid justification for going to war which is compatible with contemporary Just War Theory and international law. Put another way, what I have argued in this section strongly suggests that, in accord with common intuitions, the state does indeed have the 'right to fight' in defence of its citizens and territory. It follows from this, then, that soldiers have the right to fight on behalf of their states. Martin Cook expresses this relationship well when he writes:

Joining an all-volunteer military such as the contemporary American one may usefully be construed as a kind of 'contract'. There is, of course, the literal and legal contract, the stuff of recruiting, in which pay is stipulated and educational benefits are spelled out. But I mean to focus more on the implicit moral contract – the kind of 'contract' that social contract theories of the state such as those of Hobbes, Locke, and Rawls imagine.[29]

CONTRACTED COMBATANTS AND THE STATE'S RIGHT TO FIGHT

As interesting and challenging as Rodin's critique of the underlying basis of the state's right to national defence is, it's important to keep in mind that most theorists take this right for granted, and Rodin's critique is not uncontested.[30] In this section I will consider how the employment of contracted combatants fares if, firstly, a right to national defence *can* (contra Rodin) be derived via a reductive strategy, or if, secondly, a right to national defence can be derived (contra Rodin) from the common life via something like the argument I outline above.

Rutgers University's Jeff McMahan is unquestionably one of the most respected contemporary philosophers to address the ethics of armed conflict. He has argued that not only do Rodin's arguments against the reductive approach to the normative justification of the right to national defence fail, but that this reductive approach 'offers a sound foundation for a much-needed revision of the traditional theory of the just war'.[31] This is not the place to rehearse and assess McMahan's arguments, but I would be remiss if I did not consider the impact of those arguments, if successful, on the question of the employment of contracted combatants.

It is universally acknowledged that, not only do individuals have a right to defend themselves against violent attack, they also have a right to intervene on behalf of others who find themselves under such an attack, even to the extent (where appropriate) of using deadly force. Does it make a difference to the ethics of the latter case if the third party intervener is paid to do so? Cecile Fabre, for one, doesn't think so. She contends that 'individuals can hire themselves out for killing services, as well as procure such services, in so far as, by doing so, they provide some other party with the resources it needs rightfully to defend itself against an unjust threat'.[32]

Certainly Fabre's view has strong appeal. Consider, for example, the hypothetical case of Jane, who finds that she has to walk through a bad neighbourhood at night. Jane is a taxpayer, and is therefore rightfully under the protection of the local police. However, the local police are not sufficiently effective to ensure her safety. Believing (rightly) that her chances of being attacked are high, Jane enters into a contractual arrangement with a bouncer at a nightclub she happens to pass, who agrees to protect her on her walk through the bad neighbourhood for an agreed fee. As it happens, Jane is attacked, and her companion does intervene to save her and uses lethal force to do so, which is proportionally appropriate given the violence of the attack and the imminent threat of death to Jane. Do we think that Jane's companion is in some sense unethical? No. True, we might have valued his actions more highly had he offered his protection for free. But we do not consider his actions to be *unethical*. This example reflects the dynamic that exists between state police and private security guards. It has not, to my knowledge, been argued that private security guards are somehow deeply immoral because their occupation somehow violates the citizen–state relationship with respect to the employment of force. Why then, should this suddenly become an issue when military force is involved?[33] If we accept McMahan's view that the right to national defence is a derivative right based on the individual's right to self-defence, then it's hard to see why there should be any difference at all.

What of a 'common life' based approach to the justification of the state's right to national defence? Does this different approach give rise to some reason why the use of contracted combatants might be incompatible with this right? It's noteworthy that Michael Walzer, author of the most influential version of a 'common life' based approach to the state's right to use armed force,[34] makes no mention of any concern in this regard when he discusses contracted combatants in his only writing to date on this issue.[35] Instead he focuses solely on his concerns about accountability, an issue I address later in chapters 6 and 7. That's not surprising, considering that Walzer's approach is basically a variant of the social contract-based justification discussed above. But what of my own approach? As I've pointed out, one way to avoid Rodin's critique is to reject the underlying 'primacy-or-right' assumption which underpins his approach, where 'a principle ascribing rights to men as binding unconditionally' is taken as basic, but without recognizing 'as similarly unconditional a principle of belonging or obligation'.[36] If we accept, following Taylor, that there exist a set of obligations which go along with our rights as citizens, and those obligations include a responsibility to fight in defence of the state which secures the common life which is so critical to our own human flourishing, does this exclude the use of contracted combatants?

It may well be possible to argue that the rights we hold which are secured for us by the state are accompanied by obligations or duties, such as military service, which we in turn owe to the state. But even if this is so, how would employing the services of contracted combatants conflict with this? Consider another fictional analogical case. For the sake of argument, let us assume my property rights give rise to a mirror duty to others, a positive duty to intervene in defence of their property rights (as opposed to merely a negative duty not to violate others' property rights). Let us also imagine I am deeply committed to fulfilling this duty, but I also have other affairs to attend to, and so cannot give as much time as I would like (or indeed, feel duty-bound to give) for this purpose. In order to live up to what I deem to be my obligations, I give a significant portion of my hard-earned salary towards employing a security guard, whose full-time job is to patrol my neighbourhood in order to help protect my neighbours' homes and property from thieves and vandals. I have, in effect, elected to fulfil my duty by employing a proxy to take the necessary action on my behalf. Is there any reason here to think that, because I am not fulfilling this duty *personally*, I am therefore not fulfilling it at all? It's hard to see why that should be the case. By analogy, it's equally hard to see why employing contracted combatants, via democratically overseen mechanisms and using citizens' tax contributions, would somehow undermine or conflict with a citizens' obligation or duty to contribute to the safety of his fellow citizens and the functioning of the state which serves as defender of his fellow citizens' basic rights.

It seems, then, that there is little justification for the view that employing contracted combatants conflicts with the state's 'right to fight' or (if there be such a duty) the citizen's duty to contribute to the state's efforts to secure the safety and security of those under its care.

PUBLIC VERSUS PRIVATE

A significant amount of the unhappiness over states' employment of contracted combatants arises from strongly entrenched views of the distinction between 'public' and 'private'. This is sometimes expressed in terms of the idea that some functions are 'inherently governmental'. As Patricia Owens points out, this is a standard feature of the analysis of contracted combatants in international relations (IR) theory:

> In IR, 'soldiers of fortune' and the wide variety of other non-state fighting units are primarily understood in relation to states' efforts to achieve a 'public' monopoly on force and questions of what it is for a sovereign state to generate, organize and control force. In this regard, the following comments and concerns are typical. How do

'exports of private security services affect states' ability to control the force that emanates from their territory'? 'A government exercises sovereign powers.' 'When those powers are delegated to outsiders,' we are informed, 'the capacity to govern is undermined.' *The* central element of the sovereign inter-state system is broken when 'the *collective* monopoly of the state over violence in world politics' disappears. The assumption is that certain government functions are inherent to sovereignty, that sovereignty implies the ability to govern, and that the central issue for investigation is the extent of states' 'control' of the violence 'that emanates from their territory'.[37]

Owens, however, sees this conceptualization as accepting 'a historically inaccurate model of territory, population and force' and an 'ideological, rather than empirical, distinction between public and private'.[38] She is not alone in holding this view – economist Jurgen Brauer, for example, argues that 'the distinction between private and public force is arbitrarily discrete'.[39] As Owens explains

State control over the use of force ebbs and flows. Some states are so strong (and have such control) that they can allow military and security firms to operate from their territory and mobilize them to pursue their own ends. In these cases, the capacity to govern is clearly not undermined when certain features of 'sovereign power' are delegated. That the United States can mobilize forces from foreign populations through both state and, increasingly, commercial means is a crucial factor in its ability to defeat those insurgencies it defines as inimical to its political and economic interests. . . . Needless to say, while western states today choose to distinguish between public and private, those against whom they fight in Afghanistan and Iraq often possess a better understanding of the function of this distinction. As many have noted, it is only logical for insurgents to target contractors working for coalition forces and to view such attacks as part of a battle against a *political* enemy.[40]

While Owens' account is certainly messier and less theoretically satisfying than the orthodoxy she rejects, it is also clearly more accurate. Central to her view, as is evident from the above quote, is the idea that the act of delegation does not undermine control and therefore sovereignty. This is a theme I will explore in depth in chapters 6 and 7. For now it suffices to note Owens' admonition that 'We ought to speak of the rise of contract, not "private" armies, for these are not "private actors operating in the public realm of warfare". They are simply actors operating in the social and political realm of war. . .'.[41]

5   The Right to be Wrong

In a democracy, [elected] civilians have the right to be wrong.

Peter Feaver[1]

In the previous chapter I argued for states having the right to use force in defence of their citizens and territory, and that the employment of contracted combatants by states does not undermine or conflict with that right. But there is a further issue which must be considered here. It is widely agreed that the state's right to use force, derived as it is from its responsibilities to its citizens, must be exercised in a manner which ensures accountability to those citizens. Broadly speaking, this is referred to the idea of the democratic control of armed force. As James Pattison points out:

> Democratic control over the use of force is morally valuable for a number of reasons. First, it is intrinsically valuable for reasons of self-government and individual autonomy. If the U.K. population is to be self-governing, for instance, it is important that British citizens have some say in when and how *their* state wages war. Second, as claimed by democratic peace theorists, democratic control is instrumentally valuable since it leads to more peaceful behavior, particularly in relations with other democracies.[2]

One aspect of the democratic control of armed force is the issue of ensuring that elected officials (and unelected civil servants) are kept accountable to the public with regard to military operations which they instigate or authorize. This is one area that has caused a good deal of concern among those who are troubled by the employment of contracted combatants (and contractors more broadly). There is a strong argument, for example, that the large-scale use of contractors in Iraq under the Bush administration was at least in part an attempt to circumvent Congressional limitations on the number of troops which could be deployed into that theatre. Another regularly expressed concern is that the availability of contracted combatants offers a means whereby governments can avoid existing controls on their use of force by using private warriors to undertake 'black' operations. As Patricia Owens puts it, 'To define an economic activity as "private" liberates processes of wealth accumulation and circulation and separates them from democratic regulation. Similarly, powerful states can organize force in a manner that appears to be "private" and/or foreign because this reduces political scrutiny.'[3]

While this is unquestionably an important concern, it is important to recognize it is not, fundamentally, a concern about contracted combatants. Instead, it is a concern about the democratic accountability of *elected officials*. While there may perhaps be circumstances in which elected officials can avoid the various checks and balances built into most democratic systems of governance through the employment of private military companies, the problem lies with those checks and balances (and the elected officials themselves), not with the companies who might under such circumstances be legally employed in a way which nonetheless weakens or undermines democracy.

A more directly relevant concern which is regularly voiced regarding the outsourcing of armed force by states is the worry that private companies which provide military services owe their primary allegiance to the owners or shareholders of those companies, and this makes them somehow untrustworthy. At the strategic level, the concern is that the outsourcing of traditional military functions into private hands could potentially undermine what scholars refer to as civil–military relations, the (in the ideal case) relationship of subservience by the military to elected civilian leaders or 'principals'. The traditional view of civil–military relations, as defined by Samuel Huntington in his classic book *The Soldier and the State*, takes the central determinants of appropriate civil–military relations to be 'soft' factors, primarily such features as military professionalism, honour and a culture of submission to civil authority. While private military companies may display these features, there is widespread concern that there is no assurance of this. Elke Krahmann, for example, expresses this concern when she writes:

> High levels of mutual interpenetration and common identity are regarded as supportive of democratic civil–military relations because they increase the commitment of the armed forces to the defense of their society, ensure that the military shares societal norms and beliefs, and facilitate support of government policies. The model of the private military contractor undermines these historically established means of democratic control in a number of ways and thus requires a revision of traditional civil–military relations.[4]

This view is not, however, shared by all. Christopher Spearin, for example, argues that:

> The PMC-government relationship has many of the characteristics of ideal civil–military relations proposed by Samuel Huntington. As a military force, PMCs are highly trained and highly professional in the sense that their personnel (1) are knowledgeable of their field, (2) do not impress upon a government military activity against its wishes and (3) do not wish a leadership role in the daily political operations of the country.[5]

Huntington's approach has, in recent times, been challenged by a new theory of civil–military relations, one advocated by distinguished Duke University political scientist Peter Feaver, whose policy experience includes a two-year stint as Special Advisor for Strategic Planning and Institutional Reform on the National Security Council Staff at the White House. Feaver's 'Agency Theory', while acknowledging the importance of the soft factors so central to Huntington's approach, also recognizes the importance of a range of 'hard' determinants of whether military forces will submit to democratically elected civilian leadership.

I will attempt to show, in this chapter and the next, that Agency Theory is an agile tool which can advance the debate over military privatization by giving a significantly more fine-grained account of what is necessary for both appropriate traditional civil–military relations as well as what we might call civil–(private) military relations. As Peter W. Singer points out, this kind of analysis is largely missing from the academic literature:

> From its very beginning, the underlying basis of current civil–military relations theory has been fairly simple. Essentially it is a story of balancing proper civilian control with the military professionals' need for autonomy to do their jobs properly. Although ongoing debates over where exactly these lines of control should be drawn, the whole of civil–military relations theory, regardless of its viewpoint, sticks to this general assumption of a dualistic balance between soldiers and state. Presently, civil–military relations theory does not fully account for any potential role of external, third-party influences on this two-sided structure.[6]

It is critical that this analysis be carried out, in order to ensure that we avoid falling into the trap, pointed out by Musah and Fayemi, of those scholars 'who see the use of today's mercenaries (*sic*) as the effective antidote for insecurity in zones of complex emergencies, but pay little or no attention to the subversion of the very state sovereignty the mercenaries claim to protect'.[7]

HUNTINGTON AND JANOWITZ

At the heart of both Huntington's and Janowitz's analysis of the military and its relationship to the polity, is the notion of professionalism. For both, a profession is defined in a fairly conventional manner, as an occupation which has highly specialized characteristics in the areas of expertise, responsibility and corporateness. Both also restrict membership of the society of military professionals to those who belong to the officer corps. In terms of civil–military relations, Huntington takes the notion of professionalism to be at the heart of what he calls 'objective civilian control' of the military.[8] Huntington has helpfully summarized the features of objective civilian control as follows:

> This involves: 1) a high level of military professionalism and recognition by military officers of the limits of their professional competence; 2) the effective subordination of the military to the civilian political leaders who make the basic decisions on foreign and military policy; 3) the recognition and acceptance by that leadership of an area of professional competence and autonomy for the military; and 4) as a result, the minimization of military intervention in politics and of political intervention in the military.[9]

The key consequence of this professionalism-driven model is, in Huntington's account, that it provides a way to weaken the military politically (by keeping it out of political matters) while at the same time allowing it to be strong militarily, thereby ensuring both civilian control and military effectiveness.[10]

Because his focus is more sociological than political, in many respects Janowitz's approach is not a competitor but rather a complement to Huntington's theory. Perhaps the main difference between these theorists' views regarding civilian control of the military relates to their views of professional autonomy. Huntington argued for a strict separation between the values of the military profession and those of liberal civil society, and believed the imposition or infusion of liberal values into the military would undermine its military effectiveness. Writing as he was in the context of US participation in the Cold War, and with this belief about liberal values in mind, Huntington saw a real crisis looming. He believed that in a time of war the only way a liberal society can meet a serious threat is by suspending its liberal values for the period of that war. In the case of the Cold

War, which he recognized as likely to be a long-term feature of international relations, he concluded the only hope for survival was for liberal values to be jettisoned altogether, and for the US to become a conservative republic.

In contrast to this view Janowitz argued that the distinction between war and peace was becoming increasingly difficult to draw in the modern world, and that military forces were increasingly becoming 'constabulary forces' rather than the traditional warfighters of old. As a result, he argued, the professional soldier, while remaining in important ways distinct from his civilian counterparts, must become politically aware, and must of necessity therefore absorb many of the values of the society he serves. This is sometimes describes as 'subjective' civilian control.[11] He also described how the rise of bureaucratization and the increasing dependence on technology in the military produced additional constraints on the autonomy of the military professional.

What is common to Huntington and Janowitz is that for both of them civilian control of the military is assured by the military's professionalism, defined in terms of voluntary submission to civilian authorities – in Huntington's case, submission based on the incentive of civilian non-interference in the military realm; and in Janowitz's case, submission based on shared values. In this respect, then, Peter Feaver seems correct when he writes that 'The tradition inspired by Morris Janowitz provides an important counterweight to Huntington, but on the crucial question of how civilian institutions control military institutions on a day-to-day basis the Janowitzean school does not represent a significant alternative to Huntington.'[12] Narrowing the focus to Huntington's work, therefore, I will in the next section outline Feaver's theory, which I will argue represents an important advance over Huntington's approach.

FEAVER'S AGENCY THEORY

Feaver makes it very clear from the start of his book that it is the issue of maintaining civilian supremacy over the day-to-day control of policy decisions which is the central focus of his Agency Theory, rather than the question of whether or not the military is a direct threat to democratic rule. The issue of day-to-day control remains, however, a central problem for the democratic state. For while it is not its physical coercive power which causes the military to be a challenge in this regard, the military nonetheless also wields power in other forms – its claim to special expertise in military matters, the general prestige of the military, and so on. Apart from practical dangers, this also poses a danger to the fundamental principle of democratic governance – that in a democracy the citizenry by definition retains the right to decide, through their elected representatives, on all matters of state, even on matters in which experts (such as the military)[13] may have greater expertise. There are, in addition, instrumental reasons for taking appropriate civil–military relations to be important. As Steven Biddle and Steven Long have shown, harmonious civil–military relations are a significant factor in military effectiveness on the battlefield.[14]

The central difference between Feaver and Huntington is that, while not declaring these irrelevant, Feaver's focus is not on non-material determinants of behaviour (such as beliefs, norms and identity), but is instead on material factors. For Huntington, the central variable in civil–military relations is one of *identity*, the identity of the military officer as a professional.

Against this Feaver builds a model which draws on principal–agent theory, a framework widely used in economic and political analysis. Principal–agent theory seeks to address problems of agency, particularly between actors in a position of superiority or authority (principals) and their subordinates (agents). The classic example is perhaps the employer–employee relationship. Here the goal of principal–agent theory is to address the problem of how the employer ensures that the employee does what is required of him, or in other terms, how the employer ensures that the employee is 'working' rather than 'shirking'. Feaver argues that civil–military relations can be seen as 'an interesting special case'[15] of the principal–agent relationship. Because this 'special case' has unique features which are not broadly applicable to other principal–agent relationships, Feaver coins the term 'Agency Theory' to describe it.[16] This likening of the civil–military relationship to that of an economic contract is not particularly unusual. Martin Cook, for example, writes in the US context that:

> The relation between the contemporary volunteer military and American society can usefully be construed as an implicit contract. Military personnel volunteer to serve the society in the application of coercive and lethal force. . . . The terms of the contract are that the military officer agrees to serve the government and people of the United States. He or she accepts the reality that military service may, under some circumstances, entail risk or loss of life in that service. This contract is justified in the mind of the officer because of the moral commitment to the welfare of the United States and its citizens.[17]

At the heart of Agency Theory is the idea that civil–military relations are essentially a form of strategic interaction between elected civilian masters (principals) and their military servants (agents). In this strategic interaction civilians choose methods by which to monitor and control the military. What methods are chosen depends on what expectations the civilians have about the degree to which the military will submit to their authority. Submission or obedience is, in Feaver's terminology, 'working', while rebellion or refusal to obey is 'shirking'. 'The military decides whether to obey in this way, based on military expectations of whether shirking will be detected and, if so, whether civilians will punish them for it. These expectations are a function of overlap between the preferences of the civilian and the military players, and the political strength of the actors.'[18]

It is worth pausing here to consider more closely what Feaver means by the terms 'working' and 'shirking'. 'Working' is relatively

unproblematic – an agent is working when he is diligently pursuing the tasks assigned by his superior. In the case of the military,
the military is working when diligently seeking to fulfil the wishes
of its civilian overseers. 'Shirking', in this context, means more
than simply failing to work, for the military may be vigorously
pursuing military and/or policy goals, but it will still be shirking
if those goals do not correspond with the desires of the civilian
principal. As Cook points out, 'At root . . . the military does not
set the terms of its social contract – certainly not unilaterally, and
essentially not at all.'[19]

'What civilians want' is of course a complex and multidimen-
sional issue in the context of civil–military relations, far more so
than in the traditional economic applications of principal–agent
theory. Feaver observes that, in structural terms, the desires of
the civilian principal can be viewed as twofold. First, civilians want
to be protected from external enemies. Secondly, they want to
retain political control over the military, and ensure that it is in
fact the civilian principal who is making the key decisions concerning the military and its activities. Feaver calls the first of these
the 'functional goal', and the second the 'relational goal'.

In principal–agent theory terms, the problem of getting the
agent to work in the desired manner is called the 'moral hazard
problem'. Feaver points out that in the general literature on principal–agent theory, there are two distinct opinions in this regard.
On the one hand there are those who contend the best way of
ensuring that the agent is working is by applying the best available monitoring system. On the other hand there are those who
believe the superior approach is to implement measures aimed
at adjusting the agent's preferences to increasingly coincide with
those of the principal. Feaver's theory draws on insights from
both. Importantly, he adds an important additional consideration
which is seldom addressed in principal–agent theory, namely
'how agent behavior is a function of their expectation that they
will be punished if their failure to work is discovered; traditional
principal–agent treatments assume punishment is automatic but

. . . I argue . . . that assumption must be relaxed when analyzing civil–military relations'.[20]

Envisaged in this way, civil–military relations are viewed as a game of strategic interaction in which each side attempts to achieve outcomes which maximally promote their separate interests. This is clearly a significantly different approach to that favoured by Huntington and Janowitz, where non-material factors such as identity and moral commitments arguably play the central role. These factors are not, however, irrelevant to Agency Theory. Instead, Feaver argues, Agency Theory provides a framework of analysis against which the influence of these factors may be measured and assessed. In particular, they can be understood in terms of the attempt to seek convergence between the preferences of the civilian principal and the military agents.

The preference for honour, discussed in the opening chapters of this book, is one of three preferences which, according to Agency Theory, the military agent is assumed to have. Another is the preference for specific policy outcomes. This is different to the usual principal–agent relationship, where the agent generally has no interest in which economic policy is pursued by the principal. The military agent, on the other hand, has a preference for policies that do not needlessly risk his life. In addition, the military agent has a preference for policies which give overwhelming supremacy on the battlefield. The last basic military preference is one for maximal autonomy, which translates in large part into a desire to minimize civilian interference in military affairs. All these preferences can lead the military to attempt to influence policy in ways which undermine civilian control. In terms of democratic governance, this is pernicious even when such interference leads to better security arrangements than would otherwise have been achieved. Dealing with this is made all the more difficult by the fact that the military agent carries a particular moral status – his willingness to make the ultimate sacrifice for his country acts in some sense as a moral counterweight to the civilian principal's political competence. As a consequence, 'the moral ambiguity of the relationship bolsters the hand of a military agent should he choose to resist civilian direction'.[21]

The other central problem for civil–military relations, in terms of Feaver's principal–agent derived theory, is the 'adverse selection problem'. This is the problem facing a principal in selecting which agent to contract with to undertake a task. Each agent has a strong incentive to portray himself as being far more diligent than he is, in order to ensure that he is contracted, which complicates the principal's task of selecting the best possible agent for the job. In civil–military terms the task is one of leadership selection – which potential senior officers are most likely to lead the military to work rather than to shirk? The special nature of the military context gives this problem a unique twist. As Feaver seems right to point out, it is 'at least plausible' that the personality traits which confer advantage on the battlefield are by their nature problematic in terms of ensuring submission by the military agent to the civilian principal.[22] Indeed, as we have seen, this is one of the central reasons why Huntington advocates a sharp differentiation between the civilian and military spheres.

So described, Feaver's Agency Theory offers a very useful descriptive framework by which to understand civil–military relations. In the next section I consider of the main advantages which arise from the application of Agency Theory.

Agency Theory: General Advantages

The defining feature of military professionalism, in Huntington's account, is voluntary submission to civilian authority: 'A highly professional officer corps stands ready to carry out the wishes of any civilian group which secures legitimate authority within the state.'[23] This obviously raises questions about definitional circularity. Huntington's notion of 'objective civilian control', as outlined in the previous section, is defined in terms of military professionalism, while military professionalism is defined as voluntary submission by the military to civilian control. Another problem with Huntington's approach, as historian Richard Kohn points out, is that 'while "objective" civilian control might mini-mize military involvement in politics, it also decreases civilian control over military affairs'.[24]

The most obvious advantage of Agency Theory is that it intro-duces material factors (like mechanisms for monitoring and control) into the account – something which is clearly missing from the theories proffered by Huntington and Janowitz – while at the same time not excluding the non-material factors (like identity and moral commitments) highlighted by these theo-rists. That this matters is demonstrated convincingly by Feaver in the central chapters of *Armed Servants*, where he shows that Agency Theory fits far more closely with real-world civil–military relations – specifically the cases of Cold War and post-Cold War civil–military relations in the United States – than its main rival, Huntington's theory of 'objective civilian control'.

Agency Theory offers both a way of assessing the degree of civilian control of the military, as well as outlining mechanisms for addressing the constantly-threatened imbalance in the civil–military relationship. These control and monitoring mechanisms (which will be considered in depth in Chapter 7) address the issue that is at the heart of both the moral hazard and the adverse selec-tion problems, namely information. The mechanisms provide ways by which the principal can cause the agent to reveal the information the principal needs to make good decisions about its agents; or else they work by adjusting the incentives on offer to the agent in ways that can give the principal confidence that the agents' preferences are in line with those held by the principal.

These monitoring mechanisms are general features of most accounts of the principal–agent relationship, though obviously their specific application to the civil–military context is new. What sets Agency Theory apart from other principal–agent theories, however, is the close attention that is given to punishment mech-anisms. The principal–agent literature generally takes punish-ment for granted. But this is clearly significantly more difficult in the context of civil–military relations, due to the unique coercive power available to military forces. As Feaver observes, history is replete with examples of *coups* which have been triggered by an attempt to punish the military for some or other indiscretion. Thus the first question here is whether or not civilian principals can in fact punish the military. In what may be viewed as a major concession to Huntington, Feaver expressly sidesteps this question, arguing that it is not relevant in a discussion of Agency Theory, which takes as given a relationship in which the military understands itself in the role of the agent, subservient to its civilian masters.[25] Nonetheless, Feaver makes his own view of the prerequisites for punishment mechanisms in the civil–military context very clear:

> . . . the power to punish rests on a normative foundation – that is, the willingness of the military to be punished – and this normative foundation is thus a prerequisite for democratic civil–military relations. It exists in the United States and other advanced democracies but not necessarily in all countries. . . . [T]his may limit the applicability of the agency model to other countries. [26]

This is an important qualification of Agency Theory, one to which I shall return in the next section. Where punishment is a possibility, there are, Feaver argues, a wide range of punishment options available to civilians (again, these will be explored in depth in Chapter 7).

These mechanisms for monitoring and punishment represent a clear advantage for Agency Theory over its rivals, which offer no framework of this kind. In terms of analytic power, the practical value of Agency Theory is clear. Feaver is correct that 'Agency theory cues us to look for certain things and to ask certain questions in a case study and thereby illuminates the give and take of day-to-day civil–military relations in ways that a straightforward journalistic account might miss.'[27] Furthermore, Agency Theory offers a way of understanding civil–military relations which extends beyond the traditional concern with coups to the everyday strategic interactions between military agents and their civilian principals. The presumption that the military will desire to shirk – where this is understood as more than simply disobeying orders – is an important one, and emphasizes the need for civilians to be constantly vigilant. In addition, Agency Theory offers a means of systematically analysing historical examples of civil–military relations, which Feaver himself does very thoroughly in his analysis of Cold War and post-Cold War US civil–military relations.

It is also clear that Agency Theory, as outlined by Feaver, offers scope for further development, and can incorporate insights from other theories (such as Huntington's) without changing its basic structure. This flexibility is important in the context of today's rapidly changing security environment in which military forces are increasingly deployed in unfamiliar roles, with potentially unexpected results for civil–military relations. Related to this is another advantage of Agency Theory, namely that it 'preserves the civilian–military distinction – the *sine qua non* of all civil–military theory – but without reliance on an ideal-type division of labor. And it preserves the military subordination conception essential to democratic theory, without assuming military obedience.'[28]

Clearly then, there are good reasons for considering Agency Theory to be among the most useful frameworks for analysing of civil–military relations currently in existence – at least in the day-to-day strategic interactions between the military agent and the civilian principal. An important question remains, however. Given Feaver's own restrictions of the scope of Agency Theory to mature democracies where there is a normative presumption of civil control of the military, how applicable is it in dealing with the possibility of coups? My purpose in analysing Agency Theory is to assess its general utility, but with a particular eye to its possible application to private military companies. Given the genuine concern among analysts and the public that private military companies might overthrow legitimate governments, it is essential that Agency Theory be able to deal with the possibility of coups and attempted coups if it is to be of utility for this project.

Agency Theory and Coups

Because Feaver's focus is on US civil–military relations, he is careful to emphasize that his conclusions regarding the applicability of Agency Theory can only be seen as applicable in mature democracies like the US, where the submission of the military to civilian authority is a normative presumption. That disclaimer in place, Feaver also recognizes that the obvious next step for Agency Theory research is to examine whether it is applicable in less stable democracies, where the threat of coups is a real one. Although Feaver doesn't attempt any kind of systematic answer to this question, it seems his intuitions lead him in different directions. On the one hand, he stresses the connection between Agency Theory and the normative presumption of civilian oversight mentioned above.[29] On the other hand, despite his laudable conservatism in not extrapolating results beyond the scope of his investigation, he is unable to completely restrain a cautious optimism on this point:

> Agency Theory may even make some contributions to the study of civil–military relations in countries where the threat of coups is real. After all, a coup represents the ultimate in shirking – reversing the principal–agent relationship so that the old agent (the military) becomes the new principal (the dictator). Pathological civil–military interactions within the agency framework could end up in a coup.[30]

Despite this flash of optimism, Feaver immediately expresses his belief that if Agency Theory were to be applied to 'coup-ridden' states it would require significant modification. It is on this point I find myself for the first time in disagreement with Feaver. For the essence of the principal–agent relationship is that it is a 'game' of strategic interaction between two parties, where each is presumed to be seeking dominance. Thus, as long as both parties exist (i.e. where civilian government is real rather than just a front for the military), then there will be a 'game' of strategic interaction between the two, and therefore there is a good *prima facie* reason to believe that Agency Theory will be applicable. The central question is whether, under such conditions, civilian monitoring and punishment is possible. Even where it is not, measuring such cases against Agency Theory enables a clear and objective judgement about civil–military relations in that particular state to be made.

Consider by way of example the important study by Patrick J. McGowan of coups in West Africa between 1955 and 2004. His investigation led him to conclude that 'In contrast to the rest of the world, where coups became less common and less effective from the 1970s onwards, West Africa remains the most coup-prone region in the world.'[31] A significant factor in the cycle of coups in West Africa, according to McGowan, is the structure of military forces there, which tend to break down into factions. McGowan quotes Decalo, who points out that 'many African armies bear little resemblance to a modern complex organizational model, and are instead a coterie of armed camps owing primary clientelist allegiance to a handful of mutually competitive officers of different ranks seething with a variety of corporate, ethnic and personal grievances'.[32] Agency Theory offers a ready framework to see why such a military structure makes coups more likely. For one thing, such conditions make monitoring and punishment of the sort outlined by Agency Theory very difficult, and thereby increases the likelihood of shirking among the military.

McGowan's study also brings to light some interesting data on which factors seem to have decreased the likelihood of coups in West Africa. A crucial factor appears to be the quality of political leadership in the countries concerned. In this regard he writes of the recent history of Cape Verde, Senegal, Ghana and Mali as follows:

> What clearly does make these four states different from the rest of West
> Africa is the quality of their political leadership since independence

in the cases of Cape Verde and Senegal and since the coups that brought Jerry Rawlings and Amadou Touré to power in Ghana and Mali. Senegal has benefited from three presidents who rank among Africa's most accomplished statesmen: Presidents Senghor (1960–1980), Diouf (1981–2000), and Wade (2000–). It is noteworthy that President Diouf made an up-to-then-unprecedented military intervention in Gambia in 1981 to suppress what otherwise would have been a successful coup against President Jawara. Presidents Pereira and Monteiro stepped down after losing democratic elections in Cape Verde in 1991 and 2000. Pereira strongly opposed the first successful military coup in Guinea-Bissau in 1980, broke diplomatic relations, and removed from the Cape Verde Constitution provisions relating to an eventual union between the two counties.[33]

Once again Agency Theory provides a ready answer for why this is the case. Strong political leadership of the kind referred to here is exactly what Agency Theory would predict as being among the factors most likely to lead to success in the civil–military realm, given that the civil–military relationship is a strategic interaction between the civilian principal and the military agent. Furthermore, the *type* of strength involved in this leadership is important. This is not 'strong-man' leadership, but rather leadership which firmly emphasizes democratic accountability. These are precisely the conditions that optimize the possibilities for the operation of the types of material factors outlined in Agency Theory.

An important factor Feaver has overlooked is that, even in states where there is no presumption that the military will submit to civilian oversight, and where civilian governments have few resources with which to apply coercive power over military agents, these civilian governments can still put into place both monitoring and punishment mechanisms, *by means of their involvement in regional organizations*. Keeping with our African theme, consider the examples of the African Union (AU) and the Southern African Development Community (SADC). Such organizations adhere to principles and commitments which have direct impact on military subservience to civilian governments. One example is Operation Boleas, the 1998 SADC intervention in Lesotho, which was undertaken in response to a suspected coup. That intervention was explicitly undertaken to uphold a clear SADC principle rejecting the military overthrow of civilian governments. The AU has shown a similar (albeit inconsistent) commitment to this principle – in recent times, for example, Mauritania had its membership of the AU revoked following a military coup there in 2005. Furthermore, the AU has in its toolbox the African Peer Review Mechanism – under which member nations voluntarily submit to review by an AU appointed panel on 'standards and practices that lead to political stability, high economic growth, sustainable development and accelerated sub-regional and continental economic integration'[34] – which seems to give ample scope for the monitoring of civil–military relations. Punishments available to address transgressions of accepted norms of military submission to civilian authority could range in severity from military intervention to oust the coup plotters (as in the case of Lesotho), sanctions, and diplomatic censure and isolation – where coups have actually taken place – to more limited measures which affect only the military directly, for less serious forms of shirking. Examples of these limited measures might include ejection from prestigious regional military arrangements such as the African Standby Force, withdrawal of training and other assistance, and expulsion of officers of the offending military from military colleges in other countries.

McGowan, albeit cautiously, affirms a similar view from the perspective of his empirical study of coups in West Africa. In this regard he points out that:

> . . . the new African Union (AU) and the New Partnership for Africa's Development explicitly reject military coups and military rule and were able to reverse a successful coup in Sao Tome and Principe in July 2003, although such pressure did not work to reverse Francois

Bozize's successful coup in the Central African Republic in March 2003. This pan-African initiative may have discouraged some West African militaries from plotting and attempting coups. . . . [I]f foreign-aid-donor nations would cooperate with the AU and withhold aid from any country that experiences a coup, together, they could help make African coups a scourge of the past.[35]

As McGowan's analysis implies, focusing on any lack of impact of regional organizations in recent history in Africa misses the point. The point is that such actions are *conceptually possible*, and in some cases have been actualized. Punishing coups can be done – how much punishment results, and how much of a deterrent there is against coups as a result, depends on how seriously civilian principals take the threat and how much they are prepared to invest in the deterrent.

Thus there seems good reason to respectfully reject Feaver's claim that 'Agency Theory is only applicable in those settings where the military conceives of itself as the agent of the civilian; crucial to that conception is a recognition of the civilian's right to sanction, and hence an explicit commitment to submit to sanctions'.[36] More important than this is the potential for implementing monitoring and punishment mechanisms, even in cases where the military's commitment to principles of civilian oversight are limited or non-existent, and as we have seen this is a real possibility.

A further advantage of Agency Theory in the context of weak democracies lies in its value when considering attempts to 'democratize' military forces that have traditionally existed as part of totalitarian regimes. Democratization programmes, given the Huntingtonian orthodoxy, have tended to focus on inculcating a professional ethos among the officers of the military in question. While there is undoubtedly benefit to be gained from such training (which, as we saw above, can be accounted for into the theoretical matrix of Agency Theory), this can only be viewed as a long-term strategy, for such values take time to become embedded into the culture of a military force. In the shorter term, a clear grasp of the monitoring and punishment relationship described by Agency Theory can promote the implementation of practical mechanisms for oversight of the military. The presumption that a military will desire to shirk is a particularly useful one in such contexts.

Therefore it seems there are good reasons to believe that Agency Theory is flexible and robust enough to address situations in which the threat of coups is a very real one. It is clear, also, that Agency Theory represents a significant advance over the Huntingtonian orthodoxy in understanding and managing civil–military relations. With this in place, I now turn to considering what impact the privatization of armed force has on appropriate civil–military relations.

6   Contracting and Delegation

. . . any equilibria of delegation and control are unlikely to endure, giving way to new arrangements as costs and benefits shift.

Peter Feaver[1]

As we have seen, Feaver argues convincingly that civil–military relations are essentially a strategic interaction between civilian governments and the military, which elected civilians create and contract with for the purpose of protecting society from its enemies (and, we might add – beyond Feaver's own account – for the purpose of pursuing some of the civilian government's policy goals). 'It is strategic interaction because the choices civilians make are contingent on their expectations of what the military is likely to do, and vice versa.'[2] The relationship is also a hierarchical one, particularly in democratic societies where it is a core principle of democratic theory that the military be subservient to the elected representatives of the populace. The purpose of this chapter is to consider whether or not there is any substantial difference in the nature of the essential relationship between civilian principals and state military agents, on the one hand, and that between civilian principals and private military agents on the other. Critics of the private military industry have strongly expressed their reservations in this regard. Elke Krahmann, for example, expresses deep concerns over the effects of 'disconnect between military service and duty to the state',[3] while Herfried Münkler expresses the opinion that:

. . . a continuation of this tendency [towards military privatization] would have enormous political consequences, as the armed force would be subject to weak control by governments (linked only by the employment relationship). . . . Privatized warfare would rapidly take on a disastrous life of its own, in accordance with the laws of the market.[4]

James Pattison worries that a lack of control by states over contracted combatants might potentially contravene Just War Theory in a number of ways:

First, they may contravene the JWT principle of right intention themselves, given that some companies pursue financial gain rather than respond to just causes. Second, the use of private military companies can undermine the good intentions of the employing state, given the potential for discrepancy between the intentions of the state and those of the private military company.[5]

Furthermore

. . . the use of PMCs undermines one of the key justifications of the principle of legitimate authority: the limiting of the frequency and the awfulness of warfare. This is because the privatization of military force introduces a set of nonstate actors that do not fit into state-based systems of regulation. Although a state that employs PMCs is still subject to international law that proscribes certain types of behavior (such as aggressive war), the use of PMCs means that it is harder to enforce such prohibitions.[6]

In what follows I shall begin to explore whether such concerns are justified.

A key commonality between the state's employment of national military forces and private military companies, but one that is not necessarily obvious when civil–military relations is viewed outside of the Agency Theory framework, is that in both cases the relationship is one of *delegation*. This is most obvious in the case of the private military company, for the notion of delegation is built into the very essence of the commercial contract. As Feaver points out, however, the same goes for state military forces: 'In the civil–military context, the civilian principal *contracts* with the military agent to develop the ability to use force in defense of the civilian's interests.'[7] This is an important point to recognize, for the essential objection made by many opponents of military privatization is that it is inappropriate to delegate military tasks to non-governmental organizations. Peter W. Singer, for example, writes that:

> When the government delegates out part of its role in national security though the recruitment and maintenance of armed forces, it is abdicating an essential responsibility. When the forms of public protection are hired through private means, the citizens of society do not enjoy security by right of their membership in a state. Rather, it results from the coincidence between the firm's contract parameters, its profitability, and the specific contracting members' interests. Thus, when marketized, security is often not about collective good, but about private means and ends.[8]

However, once it is recognized that state military forces are themselves distinct organizations to which elected civilian governments delegate some of the responsibility of protecting the state and pursuing the state's vital interests, it is hard to see how this can stand as a meaningful objection. For delegation is the essence of democracy: citizens delegate to their elected representatives the responsibility to rule, and those representatives in turn delegate to others the specific tasks that must be carried out in order to actualize that rule. These relationships can also be expressed in terms of *contracts*, as in social contract theory. The form of the contract between the civilian principal and the military agent may look somewhat different to more standard contractual arrangements – involving as it does various cultural rituals, symbols and honours – but a contract it is nonetheless.

Feaver observes that 'The primary claim of the principal-agent literature is that delegation need not be an abdication of responsibility.'[9] This is because delegation need not mean a loss of control. As we shall see, a number of means are available to civilian principals by which to make state military agents do what they are supposed to do. In the next chapter I will examine whether these monitoring and punishment mechanisms can be applied in the case of civil–(private) military relations. Before doing that, however, it is necessary to establish whether private agents alter the fundamental strategic relationship that generally holds between military forces and civilian agents. In so doing it is important we keep in mind Deborah Avant's point that, 'There is generally some loss of control, or slippage, associated with *any* delegation; the question should not be how private choices compare with an ideal relationship, but how they compare with other available options.'[10]

What underlies the strategic relationship between civilians and the state military is the fact that there is a strong likelihood of a divergence of preferences between the two parties. This is the essence of the principal–agent problematique. Although there may at times be shared preferences among both parties, the very nature of the two-sided relationship opens up the potential for divergence. Various factors contribute to this potential: differing views of what national security goals should be, differing views of how to pursue those goals, the natural desire for the military to build the biggest 'empire' possible, the natural desire of the civilians to limit the size and scope of the military to what they deem is necessary to achieve security, and so on. As Feaver points out, 'the military has the ability and sometimes also the incentive to respond strategically to civilian delegation and control decisions – in the jargon of principal–agency, to shirk rather than to work'.[11] This defines the strategic relationship on the military's side. On the other side, the civilian principal has the desire to ensure that the military works rather than shirks, and so sets out to put in place mechanisms for making this so. Feaver sums up the results as follows:

In sum, civil–military relations is a game of strategic interaction. The 'players' are civilian leaders and military agents. Each makes 'moves' based on its own preferences for outcomes and its expectations of how the other side is likely to act. The game is influenced by exogenous factors, for instance the intensity of the external threat facing the state made up of the players. The game is also influenced by uncertainties. The civilians cannot be sure that the military will do what they want; the military agents cannot be sure that the civilians will catch and punish them if they misbehave.[12]

Returning to our central concern, we must ask the question of whether this description would read any differently if Feaver had written it about civil–(private) military relations, in which the 'players' are civilian leaders and private military agents? Feaver's account of the strategic relationship involved in 'standard' civil-military relations sounds remarkably like Peter W. Singer's account of the regularly raised concern over the trustworthiness of private contractors undertaking roles traditionally carried out by military forces:

> . . . the security goals of clients are often in tension with the firms' aim of profit maximization. The result is that considerations of the good of a private company are not always identical with the public good. For privatized peacekeeping, the ensuing dangers include all the problems one has in standard contracting and business outsourcing. The hired firms have incentives to overcharge, pad their personnel lists, hide failures, not perform to their peak capacity, and so on. The worry, though, is that these are all now transferred into the security realm, where people's lives are at stake.[13]

Given that Agency Theory is derived from principal–agent theory developed in the context of commercial relationships between employers and employees, and that this is essentially the same kind of relationship as applies between civilian leaders and private military agents, there seems very little reason to think that the strategic relationship should be any different. The only significant difference between the state military and private military companies in this context is that there is generally only one official state military for any particular country (albeit one usually divided into different services), while there is potentially a plethora of private military companies competing for state contracts. If anything, however, this difference favours the private military companies when it comes to the application of Agency Theory. As Feaver observes, there is something anomalous in applying principal–agent theory to the issue of civil–military relations because, 'There is not really a market of agents; the civilian cannot hire from many different militaries to do its work. The principal can create new military agents, and does so from time to time, but there is something of a monopoly in providing security.'[14] Feaver argues implicitly, and I believe successfully, that this anomaly does not undermine the applicability of the principal–agent framework to the sphere of civil–military relations. But it is worth noting that no such anomaly applies to the relationship between private military agents and state employers. Instead the latter relationship is a classic case of principal–agent interaction.

In broad terms then, it seems that the basic strategic relationship between civilian principals and state military agents is not significantly different to that between civilian principals and private military agents. In the next section I consider the specific goals civilian principals have in the context of military force, and evaluate whether there is any significant divergence here between what civilians want from state military forces on the one hand, and private military forces on the other.

FUNCTIONAL AND RELATIONAL GOALS

The central challenge presented to civilian principals by the nature of the strategic relationship at the heart of civil–military relations is the danger that military shirking will lead to significantly 'suboptimal arrangements' ranging from battlefield collapse, unwanted wars and coups, to simply placing an unwarranted economic burden on society. This problem is minimized when there is a convergence of preferences between civilians and their military agents. This can sometimes be achieved through, for example, promoting senior officers who have shown themselves to share the preferences of their civilian masters. Feaver, however, argues that there are limits to how far this goes:

> For starters, military communities have strong identities that mark them as 'different' from those of civilians, and this is deliberately cultivated and signified through uniforms, oaths of office, rituals, and so on; there is, in other words, some irreducible difference between military and civilian, and this will naturally extend to different perspectives. Moreover, the civil–military difference is compounded by the different role each plays, one as principal, the other as agent; there is a *de minimis* difference in perspective that attends agency, hiring someone else to do something for you.[15]

The range of monitoring and punishment mechanisms I will focus on in the next chapter are designed to address this unavoidable problem in civil–military relations. But a prior question that must be addressed is that of just what goals civilian principals have with which they desire military agents to comply. Feaver singles out two central goals which it can be presumed civilian principals have with regard to military servants: 'Civilians want protection from external enemies *and* want to remain in political control over their destiny.'[16] As we saw in the previous chapter, Feaver calls the first of these goals the functional goal, and the second the relational goal. These goals can be further broken down as follows:

The functional goal includes:

1. whether the military is doing what civilians asked it to do, to include instances where civilians have expressed a preference on both the 'what' and the 'how' of any given action;
2. whether the military is working to the fullest extent of its duty to do what the civilians asked it to do;

3. whether the military is competent (measured by some rea-
sonableness standard) to do what civilians asked it to do.

The relational goal includes:

1. whether the civilian is the one who is making key policy decisions (i.e., no de facto or de jure coup) and whether those
decisions are substantive rather than nominal;
2. whether the civilian is the one who decides which decisions
civilians should make and which decisions can be left to the
military;
3. whether the military is avoiding any behaviour that undermines civilian supremacy in the long run even if it is fulfilling
civilian functional orders.[17]

Returning to our central quest, we must ask at this point whether
there is anything different here if we substitute private military
companies for state military forces?

While the desires civilian principals have for the behaviour
of private military agents appear to be little different from the
desires they have for the behaviour of state military agents, there
are clear differences between the preferences of state militaries
and those of private military forces. One important difference
arises from the fact that private military companies are only paid
when they are deployed, while state militaries are paid even
when they are not employed in their primary warfighting role.
In terms of the strategic game described by Agency Theory, the
ideal situation for the state military is where civilians view the
environment as a threatening one and fund the military accordingly, but where the military does not in fact have to deploy or
fight, thereby avoiding all the costs incurred. As I put it in the
previous chapter, the military agent has a preference for policies
that do not needlessly risk his life, as well as for policies that give
overwhelming supremacy on the battlefield. Feaver points out
that this results in a danger that state militaries will use their advi-

sory role to pump up estimates of what military power is required to resist possible threats, while also using their advisory role to minimize the number and extent of their actual deployments. As Feaver puts it, 'There is an exceedingly blurry line between advising against a course of action and resisting civilian efforts to pursue that course of action. Sometimes negative advice can rise to the level of shirking, especially if the advice is exaggerated.'[18]

Following the same strategic logic, it appears that private military companies will be inclined to shirk in the other direction. As they are paid to deploy and receive no income from the state when not deployed, they are likely to be prone to downplaying the likely cost of intervention while at the same time exaggerating the benefits thereof. Thus, where the state military is strategically inclined to shirk in the direction of inertia, the private military company is inclined to shirk by seeking to deploy more often than is in fact necessary. Some commentators express concern over what they see as the broader implications of this. Musah and Fayemi, for example, argue that 'it is in the interest of the new mercenaries that the world remains in a perpetual state of instability' and, as a result, 'their "solutions" are often short-term'.[19]

Does this difference amount to a significant problem when considered from the perspective of the civilian principal? I argue that it does not. The first point to note is that both preferences, if carried through, result in shirking, and so there is no difference in the *type* of problem these preferences potentially raise. In both cases the civilian principal has a duty to be aware of these preferences and their potential dangers, and to act to ensure that those potential dangers do not become actual. Thus, for example, a civilian principal who is aware of the private military company's potential to exaggerate the benefits of military action can employ another company to act purely as an advisor on these matters – i.e. the latter company will gain no benefit if a decision is made to deploy. The fact that the private provision of military services is competitive and involves numerous players in a market offers the civilian principal greater flexibility of this kind than when dealing with the monopoly agent that is the state military force.

A second relevant point here is that, given that in a democracy civilians 'have the right to be wrong', there should in a democratic society be a preference for agents that will be more responsive to civilian directives. Given that, as we have seen, the strategic preference of the state military is well-paid inactivity, while the strategic preference of the private military company is active employment, there seems to be at least a small reason to prefer the private agent in this regard. Of course, this point cannot be made without an acknowledgement of the fact that in practice governments have outsourced military functions to the private sector in order to circumvent limitations that would otherwise apply to them. As James Pattison points out:

> . . . governments can employ PMCs to bypass many of the constitu-
> tional and parliamentary constraints on the decision to send troops
> into action. Using private companies gives the government more
> scope to initiate war covertly or to extend the size of state involve-
> ment without public debate beforehand. For example, PMCs were
> employed in Bosnia to circumvent the cap of 20,000 U.S. troops
> imposed by Congress. The use of PMCs can make military operations
> more palatable to domestic publics, since contractor casualties rarely
> make the headlines and are not counted in official death tolls.[20]

This is certainly a concern, and one that should be taken very seriously. But what critics of the private military industry too often miss is that the problem here lies not with the outsourcing of force *per se*, but rather with the mechanisms that are in place which are intended to keep the Executive accountable to the elected representatives of the US populace. This nefarious use of the private military industry is *symptomatic* of a deeper problem with the democratic structures that are in place, and it is those structures which need to be addressed rather than the private military industry.

A related point that favours the use of private military agents by civilian principals is the fact that private military agents have no special societal status, unlike their state military counterparts. As we saw in the previous chapter, the state military agent has a unique moral status in society, as a result of his willingness to make the ultimate sacrifice for his country. This can give the state military agent leverage should he seek to resist civilian direction. In Feaver's words, 'the moral ambiguity of the relationship bolsters the hand of a military agent should he choose to resist civilian direction'.[21] The private military company has no such moral status, despite potentially carrying out precisely the same missions, and carrying precisely the same level of risk as the state military. Once again it seems that the private military agent is, at least in principle, likely to be more responsive to civilian direction than the state military agent.

As we saw in the previous chapter, there are two further preferences that the state military agent is assumed to hold by Agency Theory. The first is the preference for honour. As I considered this in Chapter 3, I will not address this issue in depth here. It is however worth making one additional point on this matter. As Feaver observes, 'Honor permeates the famous concept of small-group cohesion, the factor that makes human beings willing to risk their lives.'[22] Numerous authors argue that the heart of small-group cohesion in military forces is commitment to one's comrades in the group, rather than commitment to broader ideals.[23] If this is indeed true, then there is little reason to think that private units will by their nature lack the cohesion necessary for battlefield success.

The final essential preference displayed by the state military is the preference for maximal autonomy. In Agency Theory terms, this autonomy acts as a substitute for profit sharing. Autonomy is what the state military receives in exchange for obedience to the civilian principal – this is the heart of Huntington's notion of 'objective control'. But as we saw previously, Kohn points out that 'while "objective" civilian control might minimize military involvement in politics, it also decreases civilian control over military affairs'.[24] It can also be counter-productive. For example, as Thomas Bruneau and Florina Christiana Matei point out,

> When the Colombian Armed Forces were left to their own, based on an understanding during the return to democracy in 1958, with minimal civilian control, they emulated the US, with whom they served in the Korean Conflict in the 1950s, and bought equipment and trained as though they were the US, rather than a developing country confronting violent domestic insurgents. Meanwhile the guerrillas, especially the Revolutionary Armed Forces of Colombia (FARC), increasingly took control over large sections of the country, stimulating the emergence of a competing body of paramilitary organizations, which resulted in a spiral of violence that made Colombia all but ungovernable.[25]

These issues are significantly less problematic in the case of the private military company, where it is profit rather than autonomy that is the key preference. While this does not mean that autonomy is not a value for the private military agent, there is good reason to expect that the private military agent will be willing to trade autonomy for profit, thereby potentially increasing civilian control. Once again, therefore, it seems that the private military agent looks somewhat better than the state military agent from the perspective of a civilian principal who is aware of Agency Theory.

INFORMATION ASYMMETRIES, ADVERSE SELECTION AND MORAL HAZARD IN CIVIL–MILITARY RELATIONS

> Principal–agent relationships involve information asymmetries. Both sides share common information; in the civil–military context, they know who the domestic players are, the size of the defense budget, the general identity and nature of their enemies. They also share a common history and political memory. But each has private information that is discerned only dimly by the other.[26]

In the case of civil–military relations, the private information held by state military forces includes expert knowledge on issues like weapons system capabilities, tactics, logistics and morale, as well as inside knowledge regarding the general attitude within the military towards the directives of the civilian principal. For civilians, the private information includes insight into political realities and preferences. Overall, however, as Feaver points out, 'information asymmetries favor the [state] military agent'.[27] This is particularly so when the state military is deployed and engaged in combat operations – the very nature of distant and chaotic engagements makes it extremely difficult for civilians to monitor the military.

Is the information asymmetry between state military forces and civilian principals matched by a similar asymmetry between private military companies and their state employers? Certainly, at the most basic level, the question must be answered in the affirmative. As Feaver implies in the quote at the beginning of this section, the very nature of the principal–agent relationship ensures the existence of some informational asymmetry. But there are significant differences between the private military company and the state military force that suggest that the asymmetry might be less pronounced in the case of the private military agent. For one thing, as discussed in the previous section, the substitution of autonomy for profit in the case of the state military force increases the likelihood that the state military force will be more resistant to civilian monitoring than will the private military company. For another thing, the nature of the market for the private provision of force increases the incentive for private companies to seek to earn the trust (and therefore the contracts) of the civilian principals by making themselves as open to the civilians as possible. Christopher Kinsey, for example, argues that the future success of private military companies will be determined more on how much 'corporate social responsibility' they display than on their ability to find new markets.[28] Avant agrees: 'Conceptions of proper behavior, such as the codes of conduct and standards in vogue among advocates of corporate social responsibility, can be important in setting expectations and norms within which the market works.'[29]

Apart from information asymmetries, principal–agent interactions in general, and civil–military relations in particular, are also afflicted by the adverse selection problem and moral hazard. As Feaver explains:

> Adverse selection refers to the moment of hiring in the employer metaphor. Has the employer hired someone who is naturally a hard worker or has he been deceived by the interview and hired a lout? Just how closely aligned are the preferences of the agent and the principal? The adverse selection problem means, in the first instance, that the employer cannot know for certain about the true preferences and capabilities of the applicant. But adverse selection is more than mere uncertainty about the applicant. It also refers to the fact that the very act of hiring creates perverse incentives for the agent to misrepresent himself, which thereby increases the chances that the principal will hire a lout: it is hard to verify the true type, and the lout has a great incentive to appear even more attractive than a good worker. . . . More generally, adverse selection can extend beyond the hiring phase to include all those situations in which the agent presents himself, or some proposal, to the principal for approval or decision. For instance, it means that because of their informational advantage over superiors, subordinates tend to propose policies that benefit their own interests rather than the interests of the superiors.[30]

While adverse selection does not confront the traditional civil–military relationship in a direct way, given that the civilian principal is not faced with a choice as to which agent to employ, Feaver observes that in this context the problem appears when civilians decide on which military officers to promote to senior rank. There are particular difficulties here because the personality of a person who is likely to succeed on the battlefield is not one that succumbs comfortably to oversight by civilians who, in military matters at least, are in all likelihood his inferiors. As Feaver observes, 'One of the major concerns of traditional civil–military relations theory was precisely the great divergence of viewpoint between what Huntington called the liberal civilian ideology and the military mind.'[31]

The other area where adverse selection appears in the traditional civil–military relationship is in the budget process, in which the civilian 'selects' what warfighting capability it will pay for, on the basis of proposals put forward by state military organizations. 'Again, because the military has an information advantage it can advance artfully drawn proposals that appear to meet civilian needs but in reality are tailored to its own interests. In the extreme, adverse selection might lead civilians to adopt policies they think will increase the military's ability to protect society but that in fact will increase the ability or even the propensity of the military to undermine society.'[32]

Peter W. Singer, for one, thinks that the adverse selection problem is particularly problematic for states that employ private military companies:

> This issue of adverse selection becomes particularly worrisome when placed in the context of the industry, with its layers of moral hazard and diffused responsibilities. Thus, even if [PMCs] are scrupulous in screening out their hires for human rights violations (which is difficult for a firm to accomplish, given that most of its prospective employees' resumés do not have an 'atrocities committed' section), it is still difficult for them to monitor their troops in the field completely.[33]

I will examine the specifics of monitoring in the next chapter. For our purposes here the interesting question is whether the fact that adverse selection is only indirectly applicable to traditional civil–(state) military relations (because of the state military's monopoly on the provision of military forces) is something that shows that Agency Theory's applicability to private military companies is limited?

Once again, the obvious rejoinder is that it is the relationship between the private military company and its civilian state employer that is the paradigm case of the principal–agent relationship, and it is the traditional civil–(state) military relationship that must be manipulated somewhat to fit this framework. The adverse selection problem very clearly applies when the state is choosing which private military company to employ, in exactly the same way as it applies when the state is choosing which contractor of any type to employ. This problem is exactly that, a problem. But as Feaver makes clear, it is a problem that applies in the context of state military forces as well, and it is one which, in that context, can be addressed by some or all of the mechanisms I will consider in the next chapter. It remains to be seen whether the same or similar endeavours on the part of the civilian principal will successfully address the problem as it appears in the civil–(private) military context.

I come finally, and most briefly, to moral hazard:

> Moral hazard refers to the behavior of the employee once hired. Like adverse selection, moral hazard refers at a general level to the problem that principals cannot completely observe the true behavior of the agent and so cannot be certain whether the agent is working or shirking. It has an additional specialized meaning based on the perverse incentives in the agency relationship. Employees have an incentive to shirk rather than work; if you can get paid for doing less, why do more? The principal, of course, tries to minimize shirking because it is inefficient.[34]

Moral hazard afflicts the civil–(state) military relationship in a more direct way than adverse selection. Because moral hazard is structurally very similar to the adverse selection problem, albeit applied downstream, it seems clear that the comments made above apply equally well here, so I will not labour the point by repeating them. Suffice it to say that there seems no particular reason to see the moral hazard problem as being intrinsically worse in civil–(private) military relations than in civil–(state) military relations.

In sum, what is missed by many critics of private military

companies is that their concern over the impact of military privatization on civil–military relations ignores the fact that civil–military relations are by their very nature fraught. As we have seen in this chapter, it appears that not only do private military companies not fundamentally part company with state military forces over the nature of their relationship with civilian principals, but on some counts private military agents also fare slightly better (from the perspective of the civilian principal) within that relationship. Better, that is, from the perspective of a broad strategic analysis. It may well turn out, however, that things look less rosy for the private supplier of military force when the crucial and more specific issues of monitoring and punishment are considered. It is to that task I turn in the next chapter.

7 Command and Control

'A central premise of political applications of the principal–agent framework is that despite all of the foregoing problems, political control does not end with the delegation decision. Civilians still have the means available with which to direct the military and thereby mitigate the adverse selection and moral hazard problems inherent in delegation.'

Peter Feaver[1]

In this chapter we consider whether the private military company can be controlled in a similar way to the state military force. Concerns in this respect abound, as Singer illustrates:

> Public military forces have all manner of traditional controls over their activities, ranging from internal checks and balances, domestic laws regulating the activities of the military force and its personnel, parliamentary scrutiny, public opinion, and numerous aspects of international law. [Private military companies], however, are only subject to the laws of the market. . . . Other than its shareholders, there are no real checks and balances on a [private military company].[2]

Whether or not private military companies can in principle be controlled is something I will explore in this chapter. It is however worth noting from the outset that one of the reasons some states have turned to private military forces is precisely because of difficulties in controlling *state* forces. Eboe Hutchful, for example, writes that:

... the phenomenon of the privatization of force paradoxically also reflects the security needs of the state itself, given its historically problematic (and declining) ability to project force; private armies ... may replace or supplement official armies, which have proven to be difficult to control politically, as well as unreliable on the field of battle.[3]

Of course it may turn out that 'private armies' are by their nature even more difficult to control than state forces. It is to an analysis of this question that I now turn.

MONITORING

We saw in the previous chapter that Feaver outlines six main means by which civilians can monitor state military forces: restricting the scope of delegation; contractual incentives; screening and selection mechanisms; 'fire alarms'; 'police patrols'; and revocation of delegated authority. In this section I will examine each of these in turn and assess their applicability to the case of civil–(private) military relations. Singer expresses a widespread concern in this regard when he writes:

> Lost oversight is the first issue of concern. When governments engage in official military and foreign policy endeavors, the policy is held accountable by a wide range of supervision, both from within their own agencies and in the competitive branches of government, such as the legislative and the judiciary. The result is a balance that keeps each branch within the law and holds their relative power in check. . . . [T]his particular form of privatization removes military expertise from the realm of public accountability.[4]

Because the focus of this book is on a conceptual analysis of the broadly moral implications of the outsourcing of armed force, I will not here consider such issues as the cost to principals of the various monitoring mechanisms discussed. As Feaver observes,

'Like traditional principal–agent oversight mechanisms, these measures are costly in terms of civilian attention (not to mention dollars) but can mitigate somewhat the informational asymmetries in the civil–military relationship.'[5] If, as I contend, this analysis shows that similar monitoring mechanisms are available to the civilian principal in asserting control over private military companies, then it seems likely that there will be considerable costs in operationalizing these mechanisms as well. It is a matter of practical policy and prudence, rather than conceptual analysis, whether or not civilians choose to pay the price necessary to have control over their military agents (whether state or private), and what degree of control civilians will consider to provide the optimal balance between cost and outcome. One point is clear from the beginning – governments that choose not to engage with the private military industry give up any chance whatsoever of monitoring or controlling it. As Deborah Avant puts it: 'Governments that have chosen to reduce their reliance on the private sector for sovereign tasks (such as South Africa) have abandoned their capacity to affect the development of the market's ecology.'[6] Christopher Spearin, Associate Professor of Defense Studies at the Canadian Forces College, argues likewise that 'Removing or preventing PMCs from operating does not remove the demand for the services they offer. Developing countries in particular will simply find other PMCs, but probably in countries whose human rights records may, at the very least, be questionable.'[7]

Restricting the scope of delegation to the military

This form of monitoring depends on the degree to which civilians are prepared to take on some of the tasks involved in tasking and mobilizing the military. This ranges from devising strategy, at the upper end, all the way down to determining specific tactics in small-unit engagements (US President Lyndon B. Johnson notoriously picked out specific bombing targets during the Vietnam War). Technological advances in areas such as communications, command and control systems, satellite reconnaissance assets and unmanned aerial vehicles all offer the civilian principal far greater potential for control of this kind than has ever before been possible. There are of course dangers here. Apart from the enormous cost of providing for civilian oversight of every military move, there is the not insignificant danger that civilians will not have the necessary competence. As Feaver warns, 'In the extreme, overmeddling could so jeopardize the lives of the military, or the fate of the mission, that the military would turn in revolt.'[8] On the other hand, stepping right back and letting the military make every decision would amount to a de facto coup, and would also not be an acceptable arrangement.

In the state military context this form of monitoring is achieved by means of such mechanisms as rules of engagement, standing orders, mission orders and contingency plans.

> Rules of engagement, in principal–agent terms, are reporting requirements concerning the use of force. By restricting military autonomy and proscribing certain behavior, rules of engagement require that the military inform civilian principals about battlefield operations whenever developments indicate (to battlefield commanders) that the rules need to be changed.[9]

Rules of engagement and such mechanisms as 'commander's intent'[10] also play another critical role, that of ensuring unity of effort on the battlefield. In Thomas Ricks' important account of the so-called 'surge' in Iraq under the command of General David Petraeus, armed contractors come in for significant criticism for having behaved in a way that was considered to be undermining the new 'population centric' approach to the war that Petraeus and others ushered in. The new approach put an emphasis on securing the population (as opposed to killing the enemy) and winning their respect. In contrast, according to Ricks' account:

> . . . security contractors behaved . . . brusquely, leading Iraqis to loathe them. The bodyguards were notorious for moving around

Baghdad without regard for other cars or even pedestrians, driving on the wrong side of the road and even on the sidewalks. Ann Exline Starr, a former advisor to the American occupation authority, recalled being told by her protectors, 'Our mission is to protect the principal at all costs. If that means pissing off the Iraqis, too bad.'[11]

This is clearly a significant cause for concern, and one that is frequently raised by opponents of the private military/security industry. But it is also an issue that is usually not properly understood. For one thing, those who raise concern on this issue often use it to condemn the contractors themselves, labelling them as ill-disciplined 'cowboys'. But as Ricks rightly points out, 'in the first several years of the war, when commanders put "force protection" above all else, there wasn't much daylight between the approach taken by the U.S. military and the private trigger pullers'.[12] Thus it was only in early 2007, when the priority of the US forces officially changed from killing insurgents to protecting Iraqis (and for many US military units and personnel it took quite some time for the change to reflect in their daily operations) that the security contractors' approach stood out and came in for criticism.

The other misunderstanding that abounds here is that it is the contractors themselves that should be criticized for not operating in line with the operational concept defined by the overall military commander. But the fact is, like state military forces, private military companies and their employees can be (and are) monitored by restricting the scope of delegation. In the latter case, this is usually done through general 'rules for the use of force' (RUFs) and more specific contractual arrangements. These rules and contracts set the scope of what the private military company must, can, and cannot do. When changing environmental conditions require these restrictions to be amended, contracts must be renegotiated, thereby alerting the military leadership and, in turn, the civilian principal, to battlefield conditions and the behaviour of the private military/security contractors. As with the state military, it is ultimately up to the elected civilian leadership to decide on how tight the restraints set by the contract are.

Contractual incentives

In the broader context of principal–agent theory, one of the key means of control available to the principal to control the agent is that of building performance-related economic incentives, such as profit sharing, into the contract which establishes the principal–agent relationship. Given that the civil–(state) military relationship is not one to which this sort of economic incentive can be directly applied, one or more proxies must be found.[13] One option, as Feaver points out, is 'slack', which is:

> . . . the difference between the actual budget appropriation and the minimum cost of providing the service. Slack can be used to buy things that the agent (bureaucrat) wants, like new equipment, perquisites, and so on, but does not actually need to provide the service. In this way, the agent has an incentive to be efficient in providing the desired service, since he can spend the slack on things he values.[14]

But, says Feaver, slack offers no real guarantee that the agent will perform as the principal desires, and requires the principal to consistently overpay for services rendered.

If slack is problematic, then the next closest proxy to profit sharing in Agency Theory is autonomy:

> Autonomy is slack without a monetary denomination. Since monitoring mechanisms vary in their degree of intrusiveness, and assuming that the military prefers less intrusive means, civilians have a powerful incentive with which to influence military behavior: offer to use less intrusive means to monitor military agents. Indeed this is how traditional civil–military relations theory treats autonomy.[15]

This is certainly true, but, as we saw in the previous chapter, it must be noted that autonomy is at best a problematic means for exerting control. In fact what it amounts to is a trade-off between a loss of control over some aspects of military life in exchange for an increase in control over other aspects of the military. In some cases, as in the example of Columbia I highlighted in the previous chapter, this can lead to near disastrous outcomes.

No such trade-off is necessary in the case of the private military company. While all organizations value autonomy, the central value of the private military company is profit. There is therefore every reason to think that the private military company operating in a competitive environment will be quite prepared to trade autonomy for profit. Thus control is not simply shifted from one area to another, but increased overall. Avant points out some of the broad advantages of contractual incentives when she writes:

> State leaders can also use markets to generate social control. . . . Not only do state purchases of security services affect the incentives for [private military companies] to reflect that state's interests abroad, they also communicate the state's values and standards for proper behavior by a [private military company]. Through procurement and other efforts to set and communicate standards and educate the private sector as to the proper modes of security service provision, then, states can also influence the ecology of the global market for security services. States that choose not to participate in these efforts essentially give up this influence ...[16]

Screening and selection mechanisms

Screening and selection mechanisms represent a 'slightly more intrusive form of monitoring' and seek to ensure that only agents with the appropriate qualities are allowed to '[enter] into the contractual relationship. This directly addresses the adverse selection problem, but it may be thought of as a relatively unintrusive information-gathering device. The way to make sure you have not hired a lout is to identify the characteristics of people who are *not* louts and then hire only them. Once you "know" the type of agent you have, you should be able to predict his behavior with greater confidence.'[17]

Once again this mechanism in the general principal–agent framework is not directly available in the civil–(state) military relations context, where the state military has a monopoly on the supply of military force. In a few exceptional cases civilian governments are in a position to choose between similarly-capable branches of the military. In the US case, for example, the Marine Corps is a meaningful alternative to the Army for land warfare, Army Aviation's helicopter and transport assets can compete in some areas with the Air Force, and Navy and Marine Corps Aviation can also compete with the Air Force. An interesting case in point was the Vietnam War deployment of Marine Corps units in roles that many contended were better suited to Army units. But choice of this kind is unusual and limited, and should be seen as the exception rather than the rule. And so, a proxy is needed in order to apply principal–agent theory to the specific case of civil–military relations. The proxy in this context is accession policy, the screening and selection of recruits and the promotion of personnel who show themselves to share civilian preferences. The latter has, of course, its limitations. 'Changes of administration can result in changes in the degree of convergence between the officers appointed by a previous administration and the incoming civilian leaders.'[18]

Related to accession policy is organizational culture. Military organizations, at least the established military organs of developed-world countries, are perhaps unique in the degree to which a culture of obedience is a fundamental feature of the organizational culture. This is definitely an important feature of ensuring that state military forces 'work' rather than 'shirk'. Nonetheless, it seems clear that Feaver is right when he concludes that 'Compared with agency relationships in other sectors of the bureaucracy . . . civilian principals have less discretion in using screening and selection to choose military agents.'[19] Furthermore, the exception clause above is important. The military forces of new and emerging democracies more often than not lack this culture of obedience',[20] and as a result many developed-world attempts to 'professionalize' military forces in such countries focus on trying to 'inject' this culture of obedience (which took generations to develop in their own militaries) into the newcomers. Such efforts are often not particularly successful, however, and it is clear that accession policy and organizational culture are rather limited proxies for more traditional and direct screening and selection mechanisms.

This is simply not the case with private military agents. In a competitive market for force, civilian principals have genuine choice regarding which agent to contract with, and the screening and selection mechanisms available to them are precisely the same as those generally available in the commercial marketplace. This, at least conceptually, provides civilian principals with far greater flexibility in choosing an agent to do their bidding. Instead of each new administration being 'stuck' with the state military institutions it inherits, in the case of private firms the option is available to contract with an entirely new batch of private military companies. This point is not lost on the industry itself. Jeremy Scahill reports in his book on Blackwater that in 2004,

> Blackwater executives, led by [founder Erik] Prince, had poured money into Bush and Republican party coffers and clearly viewed the reelection as great for business . . . On November 8, [Blackwater executive] Gary Jackson sent out a celebratory mass e-mail with a screaming banner headline: 'BUSH WINS FOUR MORE YEARS!! HOOYAH!!'.[21]

Another point worth making here is that the broader marketplace for force acts as a screening mechanism that stretches beyond the efforts of the individual state. As Avant points out, 'Even if the state is not concerned with international values, the firm, not the state, exercises control over the personnel it deploys. The firm is more likely to be concerned with international norms and the professional behavior of its personnel, particularly if acquiescence to these is important to its reputation (and future contracts).'[22] Because state forces do not operate within a market-place, such pressures only apply in a far weaker and indirect way to them, if they apply at all. This must, therefore, be considered to be an advantage for the private military industry.

In his analysis of possible means available to states to ensure control over private military companies, Christopher Spearin contends that 'trying to control every aspect of the industry through regulation . . . will not work'. Instead, he argues, a system of licensing (an instance of a screening and selection mechanism) is likely to reap the greatest benefits.[23]

In practice, the inadequacy of the mechanisms for the screening and selection of individual employees of some PMCs has been a cause of significant concern in recent years, highlighted by the tragic events that led to the August 2009 arrest by Iraqi authorities of then ArmorGroup employee Daniel Fitzsimons, a former member of Britain's elite Parachute Regiment accused of murdering two ArmorGroup colleagues. According to media reports shortly after the event, Fitzsimons had been employed by ArmorGroup despite suffering from 'post-traumatic stress disorder, anxiety attacks and flashbacks', apparently due to the company's screening mechanism's failure to pick this up.[24] Licensing of PMCs and the employment of other monitoring and control mechanisms discussed in this chapter provide means whereby states can minimize the likelihood of tragedies of this kind. *It is noteworthy that in the aftermath of this incident ArmorGroup dismissed three of its employees responsible for personnel screening, and employed additional screening experts to reassess the suitability of its deployed employees for service.*

Fire alarms

Fire alarms, in Feaver's taxonomy, are third parties who have an interest in the behaviour of the agent in question, and who therefore monitor the agent. When the agent is believed to be shirking, the interest-group concerned alerts the principal to the alleged misbehaviour. The most important fire alarm in the traditional civil–military context is the news media. This is one of the many reasons why a strong and independent news media is essential to a flourishing democracy. Defence-orientated 'think-tanks' are also important fire alarms, and tend to offer a greater depth of analysis than the news media and, indeed, often trigger news media 'alarms'.

In addition, Feaver singles out less formal, but nevertheless also important, groupings within the state military that contribute to this form of monitoring. In a conscription-based military, 'draftees, as resident civilians whose primary identity and loyalty is with civilian society, may be expected to sound the alarm if things are going awry'.[25] Conscription is increasingly rare among major state militaries. At the same time, however, the employment of reserve forces is on the increase, and it is at least arguable that reservists' dual identities as both civilians and soldiers also increases their likelihood of sounding the alarm when serious cases of shirking come to their attention. Another 'internal' fire alarm that can play a role is that of inter-service rivalry. Where the state military is composed of independent services (army, air force, navy, marines and the like) of relatively similar strength and standing, competition between these services can encourage them to blow the whistle on one another when they detect shirking. Being within the same overall military structures and being experts in the delivery of armed force means that services often do not have the same informational disadvantages as the civilian principals they serve. 'To the extent that the existence of separate services makes carrying out a coup that much more difficult, the services can be treated as separate sub-veto groups.'[26] This potential benefit to civilian principals is, however, balanced by the possibility that the services will collude in order to keep their shirking from the civilians, what is sometimes known as 'logrolling'. [27]

As the slew of reports in the recent news media testifies, private military companies are also subject to the wailing of this particular 'fire alarm', and this industry has also been the focal point of a number of in-depth research projects carried out by defence-related think-tanks. In some respects, however, the nature of the private military/security industry makes it harder for the news media and think-tanks to keep track of the behaviour of its constituent firms. PMCs are numerous and come in and out of existence in a way completely unlike the arms and units of state militaries. On the other hand, PMCs have fewer means at their disposal to prevent employees from communicating with the news media. Violators cannot be jailed, for example, as can state military employees who violate direct orders. Furthermore, government contracts in a democracy are generally open to some degree of public scrutiny, which gives the news media and think-tanks access to important information relevant to civil–(private) military relations. In addition, the competitive nature of the private military industry makes it essential that companies develop and maintain a publicly accessible profile.

It is an open question whether the employees of private military companies are more or less likely to operate as 'informal fire alarms' than draftees or reservists in state military forces. Like draftees, private military contractors do not draw their identity primarily from any particular group, for as commercial agents they remain always open to being employed by another company for greater reward. What *is* clear is that the market for the private provision for force presents a far greater chance of companies raising alarms about one another's behaviour than does the relatively limited competition between services. In particular, competitive bidding for contracts is an excellent mechanism by which to highlight things like exaggerated risk assessments, inflated cost estimates and the like. It has of course in recent times been noted by critics of the private military/security industry that important contracts have been awarded on a non-competitive basis, and that this undermines transparency. Again it is important here to reiterate the point that I am addressing the question of the conceptual possibility of applying Agency

Theory to civil–(private) military relations. If, in concrete policy decisions, governments choose not to avail themselves of the mechanisms for control described by Agency Theory, this in no way undermines the claim that these mechanisms are available in concept. Furthermore, if governments fail to act in a transparent manner when they employ the services of private military companies, then it is the governments that should be singled out for criticism in the first instance, rather than the companies involved.

Police patrols

> The next most intrusive form of monitoring has been dubbed 'police patrol' monitoring. This involves regular investigations of the agent by the principal – fishing expeditions, if you will, where the quarry is general information on what the agent is doing. Police patrols include regularized audits and intrusive reporting requirements designed to turn up evidence of agent wrongdoing and, through regularized inspection, to deter moral hazard.[28]

In the traditional civil–(state) military context, police patrols are usually carried out by civilian employees of the nation's Department of Defence, or equivalent. In the case of South Africa, for example, it was considered an important step forward for democratic control of the South African military that a separate Department of Defence with a minister and secretariat was created in the aftermath of the 1994 transition to democracy. Feaver points out that the size of the civilian staff of the department is a good indication of the degree of monitoring of the military by the civilian principals. Inspectors General fall somewhere between the category of 'police patrol' and that of the 'fire alarm': 'On the one hand, they are internal to the organization and have full audit authority; on the other hand, an inspector general's investigation is not a regularized audit and is usually triggered by some precipitating factor, like a leak.'[29]

While governments have been slow to designate officials specifically responsible for 'patrolling' the private military industry, there is no reason in principle why this could not happen. Once again it seems to be simply a matter of how much control the civilian principal chooses to exercise. Indeed, the controversy over the Nisoor Square, Baghdad, incident of 16 September 2007 involving Blackwater contractors provides a telling example. In the wake of this incident Blackwater became the subject of a Congressional enquiry (a police patrol), and efforts have been made to tighten up the laws under which private military and security contractors in Iraq and Afghanistan operate. Furthermore, in a literal example of civilian monitoring of the private military and security sector, then US Secretary of State Condoleezza Rice ordered video cameras to be mounted in Blackwater vehicles, federal agents to accompany all Blackwater contractors protecting Department of State diplomatic convoys, and all radio traffic involving Blackwater to be recorded.[30] Such actions are always available to civilian principals; the only question is whether or not there is the political will to implement them.

Revocation of delegated authority

The most intrusive form of monitoring outlined by Feaver takes the form of the withdrawal of some authority that was originally extended to the state military agent by the civilian principal. This can either be a complete withdrawal (by, for example, re-delegating a particular area of responsibility to a competing arm of the state, such as the police or intelligence community), or a partial withdrawal, in which the civilian agent involved takes on greater powers over, for example, the planning of military operations. In a discussion of a perceived reluctance by the US military to embrace 'operations other than war' during the 1990s and early part of the 2000s, military ethicist Martin Cook lays out this issue in stark terms:

. . . army officers might decide that they are willing to pay the price of reduced force structure and funding in the name of preserving the knowledge and skills central to the core functions of combat arms. In that circumstance, if the society remains committed to conducting operations other than war, it will necessarily constitute a force for that purpose. Inevitably, some subset of military skills (organization, logistics, etc.) will be necessary to carry them out efficiently. But the agents who conduct them may wear different uniforms, share different symbols, venerated different heroes, and understand their professional motivation in fundamentally different ways than combat professionals do.[31]

In a similar way, civilian principals clearly have the option of removing responsibilities from private military companies when those companies show signs of shirking. Again the case of Blackwater presents a well-known and useful example. In April 2009, against the backdrop of the Nisoor Square incident, the US State Department announced that it was to transfer the contracts it had with Blackwater (by then renamed Xe) to a competing firm, Triple Canopy.[32]

PUNISHMENT

Feaver observes that, in the general principal–agent literature, punishment mechanisms are given little attention, and punishment is largely taken for granted. In the standard economic model punishment is relatively simple – shirking agents have financial or other penalties imposed upon them or are fired. This is not, however, so straightforward in the civil–(state) military context. As Feaver points out:

> One of the distinctives of the civil–military relationship is the fact that the subordinate is almost always more powerful than the superior. This is always true in the most basic sense of brute force. It can even be true for more tangible measures of power. The military may have

tremendous political power because it is an important consumer block in a market economy. Likewise, the military can enjoy a prestige that confers political power quite apart from any consideration of physical coercion.[33]

Given the power available to state military forces, there is a real question whether civilian principals can punish their military agents unless those agents choose to accede to the punishments. The threat of coups is a real one, and one unique to the relationship between civilian principals and their military agents, whether state or private. As we have seen, there is no particular reason to think that private warriors would be more inclined than their state counterparts to attempt to overthrow elected governments. Indeed, given that their motives tend to be pecuniary rather than political, it may even be thought that there is less of a danger of this sort of behaviour from private warriors.

Coups aside, Feaver recognizes that civilians can and do punish their state military agents, and he outlines five main means by which this can be done. As one of those means is intrusive monitoring (used as a form of punishment), and I have addressed monitoring above, I will consider only the remaining four means in what remains of this chapter. As before, the goal is to discern whether there is any important difference in the applicability of this dimension of Agency Theory to the context of the private provision of armed force.

Budget cuts and withdrawal of privileges

One of the ways in which civilian principals can show their disapproval of their military agents' shirking is by reducing or withholding funding to those agents. In the US case, for example, Congress will often punish one of the branches of the military by cutting budgets for high-prestige projects, such as the development of advanced weaponry and equipment. In a similar way the military can be punished by withdrawing some or other privilege from them. For example, President Clinton was widely perceived to be punishing the military by cutting senior military personnel out of important policy decisions during his term in office.

While private military companies do not have this sort of privilege, nonetheless it is conceivable that PMCs could be punished in a similar way. For example, a company that was contracted to offer training services to a highly prestigious unit such as the US Navy SEALs would lose considerably more than the contract payments were that contract withdrawn. Prestige is an important and valued commodity in a competitive marketplace. It is clear, in addition, that financial penalties are an obvious way to punish wayward private military agents. It is worth reiterating that this is a conceptual point. If the reality is that there is in fact no competitive market for force, then obviously this point does not apply. Certainly it is the view of some analysts that genuine market mechanisms are in fact not in place much of the time. Herbert Wulf, for example, argues that 'real competition is essential to prevent companies from maximizing their profit-seeking strategies. But in reality this competition is often lacking.'[34] Where that is true, the problem lies not with the companies themselves (except to the degree to which companies might be complicit in illegal or unethical deal making), but rather with civilian principals who fail to use appropriate competitive mechanisms when assigning contracts.

Forced detachment from the military

In the broader principal–agent context, the most obvious means of punishing a shirking agent is by firing him or her. While civilian principals do not have the option of 'firing' the state military, there is the option of dissolving particularly problematic units. For example, in the aftermath of human rights abuses by Canadian soldiers deployed on peacekeeping duty in Somalia in 1993, the unit concerned, the Canadian Airborne Regiment, was disbanded. Furthermore, there are various ways within the military career system of forcibly detaching particular soldiers, sailors, marines or airmen from the military. Options range from the US military's 'up-or-out' career path system, in which military personnel who do not achieve promotion within a set time-limit are released from service; to forcing a disgraced officer to retire at a rank lower than that achieved, resulting in a significant financial loss; to a range of administrative discharges. In the private military context the general principal–agent option of a state 'firing' the shirking firm, or directing a firm to fire or reassign problematic employees, is quite clearly available and demands no further elaboration here.

Military justice

Agency Theory recognizes a range of punishments that are unique to the civil–military context. Unlike the standard principal–agent relationship, civilian principals in a democratic state have the option of applying military-specific penal codes to their state military agents. If convicted of offences under military law (such as the Uniform Code of Military Justice which applies to US military personnel), state military personnel face punishments ranging from dismissal from the military to imprisonment to, in some extreme circumstances, execution.

It has been a source of significant concern among critics of the private military industry that private military companies and their employees are not subject to the same rigorous standards of justice as state military employees. James Pattison, for example, contends that 'there is currently no effective system of accountability to govern the conduct of PMC personnel, and this can lead to cases where the horrors of war – most notably civilian casualties – go unchecked'.[35] While this might perhaps have been true in recent times, there is no reason in principle why civilian principals cannot either put in place penal codes that apply specifically to private military companies and their employees, or else expand existing military law to cover private warriors. In fact, this is precisely what is beginning to happen. In 2006 the US Congress extended the scope of the UCMJ to ensure its applicability to private military contractors, and it has been reported that, on 2 August 2007, the US House Judiciary approved a bill which, if successful, 'would place contractors operating in support of US military operations under US criminal jurisdiction and would direct the Federal Bureau of Investigation (FBI) to stand up field units to probe allegations of criminal misconduct or abuse in places such as Iraq or Afghanistan'.[36] While it remains to be seen whether specific endeavours such as these will withstand the inevitable legal challenges that will arise, it does indicate that there is no reason in principle why civilian principals cannot use penal codes to punish private military agents for extreme forms of shirking.

In the end, given the fact that the rise of the private military/security industry, at least in its current form, is a relatively new phenomenon, we should not be at all surprised that there has been something of a legal vacuum surrounding their activities. That's how law usually works – it would be odd to have a regulatory framework for an industry before the industry even existed. Arguing against the employment of armed contractors because there have been inadequate mechanisms available by which to keep them accountable is rather like our ancestors arguing against the invention of motorized vehicles because there are no traffic laws or mechanisms by which to enforce them.

Extralegal civilian action

Beyond the more formal means of punishment outlined in this chapter, Feaver also identifies an additional category of miscellaneous extralegal punishments which civilians can apply to their state military agents. This is a set of actions

> . . . ranging in severity from private oral rebukes all the way to the infamous Stalinist purges against the Soviet military in the 1930's in which

thousands of officers were shot for suspected disloyalty to the soviet regime. An intermediate form might be a situation in which the military advisor is publicly reprimanded or denied access to the civilian leader because that leader has lost confidence in him.[37]

Given the broad and flexible range of punishments that fall into this category, there seems once again, no particular reason why private military companies cannot be punished in a similar way. In a competitive marketplace a company's reputation as a reliable and capable service provider is a very important commodity. This fact offers civilian principals a range of means by which to punish shirking private military service suppliers, for example, through such means as 'leaking' poor performance reports to the media.

ANALYSIS

Feaver sums up his assessment of the applicability of the principal–agent framework to traditional civil–military relations as follows:

> The civil–military relationship is at its heart an agency relationship, and so the principal–agent framework developed in microeconomics and already used in various political applications can be profitably extended to the study of civilian control of the military. The civilian principal establishes a military agent to provide the security function of the state, but then must take pains to ensure that the military agent continues to do the civilian's bidding. Given the adverse selection and moral hazard problems endemic in any agency relationship, but particularly acute in the civil–military context, civilian oversight of the military is crucial. Fortunately, civilians have available a wide variety of oversight mechanisms, each involving a different degree of intrusiveness and therefore each posing a different set of costs on the actors. The oversight regime is supported by a sanction regime, which provides civilians with options for punishing the military when it shirks, that is, deviates from the course of action prescribed by civilians.[38]

As we have seen in this and the two preceding chapters, there are no significant conceptual differences that result from applying the principal–agent framework to civil–(private) military relations. While civilian principals do not in practice establish private military companies in the same way that state military agents are created, they do nonetheless create a market for military force through the state's monopsony on force, and may regulate the existence of private military companies through licensing requirements. (Whereas a monopoly occurs where there is only one supplier of the good or service in question, a monopsony occurs where there is only one consumer thereof.) As with the state military, civilians must take pains to ensure that the purveyors of privately contracted force 'work' and do not 'shirk'. While the particular context of the provision of military force gives special bite to the adverse selection and moral hazard problems, this is not significantly different for private military companies than for state military forces, and in some respects may be slightly less of a problem for private military companies. In this chapter we have seen that civilian oversight of private military companies can be achieved by very similar means to those by which state military forces can be monitored, and that civilian principals have, at least in principle, a very similar range of punishments available that may be directed at shirking private military agents.

I have focused here on the application of Agency Theory to the task of ensuring the appropriate control of private military agents by the democratically elected principals of individual states. I have not attempted to address the question of how this question might be addressed at the international level. But it seems fairly clear that there is no in-principle reason why similar mechanisms could not be put in place at the global level. Indeed, as David Isenberg points out, in early 2009, 'the International Peace Institute released a study that identified five different frameworks – global watchdog, accreditation regime, arbitration tribunal, harmonization scheme and a global-security-industry club

– that go beyond market mechanisms and national regulations that can be applied to what it calls the global security industry.'[39]

It seems, then, that not only do contracted combatants not suffer from some intrinsic moral character flaw that would make them illegitimate contributors to just conflicts, but there are also no good reasons to suppose that their employment should in principle undermine the supremacy of a state's elected principals over its armed servants. In the next two chapters I look beyond the state and consider the appropriateness or otherwise of the employment of contracted combatants by and on behalf of the international community, focusing particularly on the international community's 'responsibility to protect'.

8   The Responsibility to Protect

*It isn't obvious why strangers in peril halfway across the world should
be our business. . . . The idea that we might have obligations to human
beings beyond our borders simply because we belong to the same species
is a recent invention, the result of our awakening to the shame of having
done so little to help the millions of strangers who died in [the twentieth]
century's experiments in terror and extermination.*

Michael Ignatieff, *The Warrior's Honor*[1]

It is noteworthy that even the editors of a book that is arguably
one of the publications most negatively disposed to the private
military/security industry are grudgingly willing to recognize a
possible role for the private sector, if governments and international organizations are willing to put in place oversight and
control mechanisms of the sort discussed in the previous chapter.
Thus, Musah and Fayemi write:

> Despite the consistent reservations expressed in this volume, we do
> not entirely rule out some role in conflict intervention for private mili-
> tary groups outside our preferred multilateral framework. If countries,
> out of sensitivity to public opposition to foreign deployment of their
> troops, can create and finance a special crisis force bound by the laws
> governing such a country's regular forces, they could deploy such a
> force in conflict zones under the supervision of a pre-existing multi-
> lateral force or a United Nations Observer Team with UN regulations
> for such a role.[2]

Musah and Fayemi raise an interesting issue here, the possible employment of armed contractors in support of United Nations peacekeeping, stability and humanitarian operations. In this chapter I outline the emerging norm that justifies the most morally challenging of the kind of operations that Musa and Fayemi have in mind here, namely humanitarian interventions. I then consider James Pattison's framework for assessing which potential interveners can be considered legitimate. In the next chapter I consider how a hypothetical contracted combatant force, if employed as the primary tool of a humanitarian intervention, would fare when assessed in terms of Pattison's approach.

HUMANITARIAN INTERVENTION AND THE RESPONSIBILITY TO PROTECT

In the aftermath of the Rwanda genocide of 1994, in which between 800,000 and one million people are estimated to have perished, the cry of 'never again' – last heard in the aftermath of the Nazi Holocaust – once more rang around the world. The Rwanda genocide led to a wide range of political and organizational arrangements designed to prevent a repeat of that horrific event, including the creation of an African Standby Force under the auspices of the African Union.[3] Yet, despite this, humanitarian crises of massive proportions have continued to occur – mostly in Africa – with little effective response from the international community. In the conflict in the Darfur region of Sudan, for instance, it is estimated that some 300,000 people have died, and a further 2.5 million have been displaced since 2003.[4] The less well-known conflict in the Democratic Republic of Congo which, in its most recent iteration, began in 1998, had led directly and indirectly to the deaths of an estimated four million people by 2004,[5] and many estimates suggest another million, and possibly more, may have died since then.

It would be wrong, however, to consider the changes in the

international realm that have resulted from the world's horror at the Rwanda genocide and other such tragedies to be trivial. Arguably most important among these changes has been a shift in the international community's view of state sovereignty. Since the Peace of Westphalia in 1648, the principle of non-intervention, a key foundation of the idea of state sovereignty, has held sway in international law. Indeed, it is an entrenched feature of the UN Charter. Article 2 (4) of the Charter states categorically that:

> All Members shall refrain in their international relations from the threat or use of force against the territorial integrity or political independence of any state, or in any other manner inconsistent with the Purposes of the United Nations.[6]

What has changed in recent years is a revision of the idea of state sovereignty in terms of the notion of responsibility. An important articulation of this principle was expressed in the 2001 report by the International Commission on Intervention and State Sovereignty, entitled *The Responsibility to Protect*. The report, which deliberated on the issue of humanitarian intervention in the light of experiences in places such as Rwanda, Kosovo, Bosnia and Somalia, concluded that the following basic principles ought to be applied:

> A. State sovereignty implies responsibility, and the primary responsibility for the protection of its people lies with the state itself.
> B. Where a population is suffering serious harm, as a result of internal war, insurgency, repression or state failure, and the state in question is unwilling or unable to halt or avert it, the principle of non-intervention yields to the international responsibility to protect.[7]

This 'R2P' norm, as it is sometimes called, has become a significant feature of contemporary international relations. This responsibility to protect the basic human rights of those who live within a country's borders falls, in the first instance, on the state itself. If, however, the state fails to live up to that responsibility to the extent that massive violations of basic human rights are taking place within that state's territorial boundaries, then the R2P norm (in its more robust form at least) states that there exists a duty for the international community to intervene using military force where that is proportionate.[8]

Emerging international law and international relations theory (which, like the Just War tradition, is a constantly evolving entity) arguably treats the right to national defence (and the corresponding duty of non-intervention) as a conditional rather than an inalienable right. In his report to the United Nations General Assembly of March 2005, entitled 'In larger freedom: towards development, security and human rights for all', the UN Secretary General, Kofi Annan, endorsed the Commission's findings as follows:

> The International Commission on Intervention and State Sovereignty and more recently the High-level Panel on Threats, Challenges and Change, with its 16 members from all around the world, endorsed what they described as an 'emerging norm that there is a collective responsibility to protect'. . . . While I am well aware of the sensitivities involved in this issue, I strongly agree with this approach. **I believe that we must embrace the responsibility to protect, and, when necessary, we must act on it.** This responsibility lies, first and foremost, with each individual State, whose primary raison d'être and duty is to protect its population. But if national authorities are unable or unwilling to protect their citizens, then the responsibility shifts to the international community to use diplomatic, humanitarian and other methods to help protect the human rights and well-being of civilian populations. When such methods appear insufficient, the Security Council may out of necessity decide to take action under the Charter of the United Nations, including enforcement action, if so required.[9] (emphasis added)

If Annan's comments reflect an emerging consensus regarding the applicability of the idea of humanitarian intervention, and I believe there is good reason for thinking that they do,[10] then in breaking with the notion of the inviolability of state sovereignty that was established at the Westphalia Conference (at which, crucially, the Just War doctrine was entrenched in international law for the first time), international law and its cognate, the Just War tradition, is undergoing a radical revision in the recognized justifications for the deployment of military force.

Arguably the biggest problem with the R2P norm is that the duty to intervene which emerges out of it is an *unassigned* duty. It is a duty that falls to the international community as a whole, rather than to any organization or state in particular. This is obviously problematic, and can perhaps be identified as at least one of the reasons for the lacklustre response to the current crises in places like Somalia and Darfur. What is needed is some way to determine who, in particular, bears responsibility for intervening in which particular crisis. The most comprehensive approach to answering this question yet developed is articulated in James Pattison's excellent book entitled *Humanitarian Intervention and the Responsibility to Protect: Who Should Intervene?*[11]

I should state from the outset that in his book Pattison does consider the question of under what conditions, if any, it might be appropriate for a humanitarian intervention to be conducted by one or more PMCs contracted by a state or international organization like the United Nations. He concludes that it would only be ethical to turn to PMCs under exceptional circumstances.[12] His reasons for this pessimistic conclusion are his view that:

(a) PMCs operate largely outside of the bounds of domestic and international law, and are therefore unaccountable and more prone to violate the laws and norms of the use of force; and
(b) states will be likely to fail to fulfil their duty of care to the contracted combatants fighting on their behalf.

What is immediately clear, however, is that neither of these are intrinsic features of the employment of PMCs for humanitarian interventions. As I have argued previously, there are no reasons to think that, where the necessary political will exists, contracted combatants cannot be held accountable in essentially the same ways (including, but not restricted to, legal sanctions) as state military personnel. And we might hope that, with better under-standing, states might well begin to take seriously their responsibilities to *all* those who fight on their behalf.

Setting these contingent issues aside, then, in this chapter I outline Pattison's 'moderate instrumentalist approach' to the question of who should intervene in cases of extreme and massive violations of human rights. Thereafter, in the next chapter, I turn to an analysis of how contracted combatants and the PMCs that employ them fare in the light of this approach. I argue that, contrary to the standard view, there are good reasons to think that there are conditions under which employing contracted contractors for humanitarian intervention would be morally *preferable* to employing state military personnel. I conclude the chapter by considering how contracted combatants fare in the light of the 'moral paradox of humanitarian intervention' identified by Gross and others.

WHO SHOULD INTERVENE? PATTISON'S MODERATE INSTRUMENTALIST APPROACH

There are, says Pattison, two main criteria that establish whether the conditions exist which justify a humanitarian intervention.[13] The first criterion is qualitative, and addresses the kinds of rights being violated. Following Oxford University's renowned ethicist Henry Shue, Pattison calls these 'basic rights', and includes among them the rights not to be subject to murder, rape and assault. The second criterion is quantitative: the circumstances must involve large-scale violations of those basic rights. These criteria reflect a long-standing principle of the ethics of armed conflict, that of proportionality. According to this principle the use of armed force must be proportional to the harm its use is supposed to address. Given that armed force is a blunt instrument which almost inevitably causes suffering when applied, armed humanitarian intervention should only be undertaken when the circumstances are sufficiently dire that they outweigh the suffering that the intervention itself will cause.

Most scholars now agree that humanitarian intervention is justified under sufficiently severe conditions. Far more difficult to ascertain is the question of who has the right and responsibility to intervene. Some scholars suggest that we ought not to try to ascertain this, but instead be guided by the maxim 'who can, should'.[14] But this approach is clearly inadequate and likely to lead to shirking of this important duty. Pattison considers a range of potential interveners, from the United Nations, to regional organizations such as NATO and the African Union, down to individual states. None of these, he concludes, is a 'stand out' candidate,[15] and so the question becomes one of assessing which potential intervener is the most legitimate in any particular set of circumstances. Legitimacy is not, Pattison argues, a fixed concept, but must instead be measured according to a scale. While the ideal intervener would possess full legitimacy, an intervener could still be morally acceptable if it had an adequate degree of legitimacy.[16] But which qualities of an intervener carry moral weight in making this assessment?

The moral irrelevance of an intervener's legal standing

The most common response to this question is that it is the intervener's legal standing that carries the most moral weight. Thus it is generally presumed that if an intervention is authorized by the Security Council of the United Nations, then the intervention is both morally and legally legitimate. Pattison, however, argues convincingly that the legal status of the intervener in fact carries very little weight.[17]

Pattison addresses the four central lines of argument given by those who support the idea of the moral significance of an intervener's legal status. The first is based on the idea that the authority of a legal intervener is the product of the processes by which international law is formed, in particular by state consent to inter-

The Responsibility to Protect   151

national law and the authorization of the UN Security Council. State consent, contends Pattison, is of little moral significance because, firstly, states' positions on issues in international relations are often not representative of the views of the majority of their citizens, even where the states concerned are democracies. Furthermore, the process of state consent gives a formal equality to individual states. But given the vastly differing populations of states (from those numbering in the thousands to those, like China and India, in the billion range), this cannot be considered to grant moral legitimacy. A third critical reason Pattison gives for rejecting this 'state consent' view is the fact that international law is often not created through state consent freely given, but is often the product of cajoling, bribery and blackmail by powerful nations of the kind that would be considered entirely inappropriate, were it carried out by individuals attempting to secure the 'consent' of other individuals. For similar reasons Pattison warns us not to overstate the moral weight of Security Council authorization. This powerful body is highly unrepresentative (composed as it is of five powerful permanent members – China, France, the Russian Federation, the United Kingdom and the United States – plus ten non-permanent members with limited powers), a situation exacerbated by the veto powers of the permanent five.

Pattison also rejects the view that an illegal humanitarian intervention is morally problematic because it could be a cover for an imperialist or neo-colonialist military intervention. In such a case we would not be dealing with an illegal humanitarian intervention at all, but rather an illegal non-humanitarian intervention. Related to this concern is the third main line of argument that Pattison considers, namely the 'bad precedent' view. Here the idea is that illegal humanitarian interventions will reduce the force of the norm of non-intervention, thereby increasing the likelihood that states will undertake abusive forms of intervention such as imperialism. Pattison, however, contends that this is an empirically questionable claim, and quotes with approval Mark Stein's claim that 'the idea that humanitarian interventions will lead to nonhumanitarian wars has been somewhat overtaken by events'.[18]

The last line of argument that Pattison considers (and rejects) as a possible basis for the idea that the humanitarian intervener's legal status is of considerable moral significance, is one based in the view that the international order is undermined when humanitarian intervention takes place outside of the recognized international legal framework. This is because, the argument continues, such illicit humanitarian activity undermines the existing structures that order the international system and keep chaos at bay. But this too seems overly alarmist, given that the international community does seem to condone humanitarian interventions of questionable legal status (such as NATO's intervention in Kosovo in 1999), and the structures of international order seem to have suffered no obvious ill effect as a consequence. On the contrary, Pattison argues (following Ryan Goodman)[19] that expanding the general acceptability of the humanitarian justification for intervention could well have positive effects for international order, by tying intervening states to the humanitarian justifications they offer from the onset, and limiting the potential justifications for any escalation of hostilities.

Effectiveness

If the intervener's legal status does not carry much moral weight, what does? The answer, contends Pattison, is mostly about effectiveness. While there are, as we shall see, other considerations, it is the likely effectiveness of the intervener in achieving the humanitarian goals of the intervention that carries the most weight. This intuitively compelling principle is at the heart of Pattison's 'Moderate Instrumentalist Approach'. Effectiveness is defined by the likelihood of the intervener succeeding in increasing the enjoyment of basic human rights as a result of the intervention. Because a potential intervener's legitimacy must be assessed prior to the intervention, it is the *likelihood* of being effective that matters, rather than the actual success of the intervention (though the latter will obviously affect future assessments of the likelihood of future effective interventions). Pattison's nuanced account of effectiveness addresses three different kinds of effectiveness in humanitarian interventions.

Firstly, there is 'local external effectiveness'. Here, the question is whether or not the intervener is likely to succeed in increasing the enjoyment of basic human rights in the community in which the intervention will take place. Less obvious, but also important, is 'global external effectiveness', the likelihood of the intervention not doing significant harm to the enjoyment of human rights in the international community (excluding the intervening country and the community in which the intervention takes place, which are addressed separately). This principle might be violated, for example, in a case where the intervention would lead to regional or even global destabilization which might lead to a wider conflict. Finally there is the issue of 'internal effectiveness', which assesses the impact of the intervention on the citizens of the country undertaking the intervention. As with global external effectiveness, the question here is not whether or not the intervention will *increase* the enjoyment of basic human rights in the relevant community, but rather whether or not the intervention will unduly decrease the enjoyment of these rights in that community. The latter consideration is particularly important because of the state's responsibilities to its citizens in terms of the social contract.

Overall effectiveness (the combined effect of all three kinds of effectiveness) is a necessary condition for legitimate humanitarian intervention. Given the fundamental purpose of humanitarian intervention, furthermore, in almost all real-world cases local external effectiveness will be the primary, and a necessary, condition for legitimate intervention. This reflects a widespread intuition. For example even Michael Walzer, in his critical response to the suggestion that Blackwater might be employed to intervene in Darfur, wrote 'Whatever Blackwater's motives, I won't join the "moral giants" who would rather do nothing at all than send mercenaries to Darfur.'[20]

These forms of effectiveness are assessed, in Pattison's model, according to a counterfactual calculation: is the intervention likely to lead to an increase in the enjoyment of basic human rights when compared to what would likely be the case if no intervention takes place?

The Qualities of an Effective Intervener

What, then, are the qualities of an intervener that is likely to be effective? Pattison articulates two kinds of qualities, namely direct qualities of effectiveness and indirect qualities of effectiveness. The direct qualities of effectiveness are, firstly, the possession of the necessary military resources for effective intervention. These include appropriately trained and motivated personnel, the military equipment – such as weapons, vehicles, helicopters and the like – necessary to enable those personnel to undertake their tasks, and the transport and logistical support capabilities necessary to get those personnel to the affected area and keep them adequately supplied. Non-military resources are also critical, but often overlooked (though not by Pattison). An intervener must have the political and economic resources necessary to address the underlying causes of the conflict and help build structures to ensure the long-term stability of the community in which the intervention takes place. All of this will of course be of little use if the intervener lacks an appropriate strategy and the political will to use the resources available in a committed and focused way. Pattison tellingly quotes Kuperman who points out that 'Experiences in the 1990s demonstrated that although the international community has sufficient will to intervene in many conflicts, it rarely has sufficient will to devote the resources necessary to intervene effectively.'[21]

Two further direct qualities of effectiveness that Pattison singles out are proximity and responsiveness. For reasons including vested interest and superior cultural understanding, Pattison contends that interveners that are geographically proximate are, all other things being equal, likely to be more effective. In addition, effectiveness depends in significant part on the ability to intervene at the appropriate moment in the conflict (earlier intervention being, as a rule of thumb, more likely to be effective) and being able to deploy the resources needed for the intervention rapidly.

What Pattison calls the 'indirect' qualities of effectiveness are indirect in the sense that they improve effectiveness overall (though possibly in some cases reducing effectiveness in some aspects), they improve effectiveness in the long term, and they increase the level of perceived legitimacy of the intervention.[22] Among the qualities of an intervener likely to have an indirect effect on the effectiveness of the intervention are Security Council support, following principles of *jus in bello*, and being internally and locally externally representative. Despite the lack of moral weight that Security Council authorization carries for any particular humanitarian intervention, it is nonetheless widely regarded as important, and therefore likely to increase the intervener's *perceived* legitimacy. Following principles of *jus in bello*, while sometimes a limitation on the effectiveness of the intervention, can be expected, says Pattison, to be instrumentally valuable in achieving the aims of the intervention over time. Likewise, internal and locally external representativeness (which I will discuss below) can also be considered to have an instrumental value in addition to their central intrinsic role in determining the legitimacy of the intervener.

The Non-consequentialist Criteria of Legitimacy

Up to this point, Pattison's approach to the question of who should intervene to carry out the responsibility to protect has been entirely consequentialist in character. But Pattison is careful to stress that while the likely consequences or effectiveness of the intervention are the primary consideration determining the legitimacy of the intervener, there are also non-consequentialist factors which are intrinsically important in assessing the intervener's legitimacy.

The first of these is the intervener's likely conduct – that is, the intervener's likely adherence to *jus in bello* norms. Pattison contends that we should extend the traditional view of *jus in bello* to include not only the familiar 'external' principles of *jus in bello*[23] (the norms guiding the intervener's treatment of civilians and enemy combatants), but also 'internal' principles of *jus in bello*, norms guiding the intervener's treatment of its own soldiers and citizens. The internal principles that Pattison singles out are:

> (a) the intervener should employ only appropriate combatants in undertaking the intervention (i.e. not child soldiers, or conscripted combatants,[24] or – for reasons we have already set aside – contracted combatants); and
>
> (b) the intervener has a duty of care towards the combatants deployed on humanitarian interventions (a duty which includes imperatives to provide appropriate protective equipment, medical care and the like).

The second of the three non-consequentialist factors in Pattison's moderate instrumentalist approach to deciding the question of 'who should intervene?' for humanitarian purposes, is the quality of 'internal representativeness'. By this Pattison means that there is intrinsic value in the prospective intervener's decision-making regarding the intervention being (in the broad strokes at least) representative of the opinions of the majority of the citizens of the country undertaking the intervention. While ascertaining internal representativeness is no simple task, Pattison seems correct in saying that opinion polls, referenda and even the media can provide an adequate indication of whether a state has a mandate from its citizens to undertake a particular intervention. This mandate is important because of the obligations the state owes to its citizens in terms of the social contract.

Finally, there is the requirement of 'local external representativeness'. This principle requires that the decision to intervene should coincide with the opinions of those in the community which will be subject to the intervention. More specifically, we are concerned here with the opinions of those (in the community that is the focus of the intervention) who are being negatively affected by the widespread and severe human rights abuses which provide the essential basis for a legitimate humanitarian intervention. Thus, the opinions of those carrying out the abuses, or those who give tacit or explicit approval to the carrying out of those abuses, do not count. Again, adequately ascertaining whether an intervention will be likely to be locally externally representative may be difficult, but must be considered to be possible in most cases.

A SCALAR APPROACH

These, then, are the principles of Pattison's moderate instrumentalist approach. The question remains, however, of how they are to be applied. For an intervener to be fully legitimate, says Pattison, the intervener must fulfil all of the criteria. That is, the intervener must be likely to fulfil the three consequentialist criteria of effectiveness (local external effectiveness, global external effectiveness and internal effectiveness), as well as the three non-consequentialist criteria (adherence to *jus in bello* norms, internal representativeness, and external local representativeness). Pattison recognizes, however, that available interveners may not meet all of these requirements. In that (likely) case he proposes that a scalar approach be taken, whereby what is sought is a sufficient degree of legitimacy. Effectiveness is the primary consideration here – this is the only *necessary* condition for legitimate humanitarian intervention, though it will only sometimes be also a *sufficient* condition. It is possible, therefore, for a potential intervener to fall short of one or more of the non-consequentialist requirements for a fully legitimate intervener, but for the severity

of the circumstances to nonetheless make that potential intervener sufficiently legitimate to undertake the intervention. In the
most extreme circumstances an intervener which lacks all of the
criteria except effectiveness may nonetheless be considered to
be a legitimate intervener. The question of which potential intervener, out of those that are sufficiently legitimate, has the duty to
actually intervene is answered by the principle that the duty rests
on the *most* legitimate intervener.

THE PROBLEM OF FAIRNESS

Before moving on to consider how a contracted combatant force
might fare when considered in the light of Pattison's Moderate
Humanitarian Approach, it is first necessary to raise one criticism of this otherwise excellent framework. The one significant
flaw in Pattison's approach is that it leaves us with a fairness
problem. The problem arises when the general duty to intervene
which falls on the international community at large is adjudged,
through the application of Pattison's criteria for legitimacy, to fall
to a specific intervener or coalition of interveners.[25] The concern
here is that it seems unfair for one country or organization to carry
the full burden of a duty that strictly speaking falls on all. Why
should country X, simply because it happens to be the country
which possesses the features that make it the most legitimate
intervener, bear all the costs of fulfilling a duty which falls on the
international community at large? This issue might be articulated
as a form of the free rider problem: all those countries which
fall below the level of 'most legitimate intervener' benefit from
the intervention (in the sense that their duty is fulfilled on their
behalf) while carrying none of the costs (both human and economic) of undertaking the intervention. There is a danger here
that countries which have the potential (in terms of economic and
human resources) to become the legitimate interveners might
deliberately leave that potential unfulfilled (by, for example, not

purchasing strategic lift aircraft, or equipping their military forces for expeditionary operations) in order to ensure that the burden of carrying the international community's duty to intervene falls on another nation's shoulders.

Consider, by way of analogy, the following scenario. A group of friends are frolicking in the waves or relaxing on an otherwise deserted beach, when one of their number is washed out to sea by a particularly large wave and is in danger of drowning. One of the group happens to be an excellent swimmer, so is rightfully deemed by all to be the legitimate rescuer. Once the decision is made and the good swimmer dispatched on his mission, the remainder of the group go back to their tanning and frolicking. Does such a scenario seem fair and just? My intuition is that it does not. The duty to rescue the friend in need is one which falls to every member of the group, so while it is legitimate for the best swimmer to take the lead in this effort, it is not acceptable for that person to bear the full burden of the rescue effort on behalf of all of the others. We should expect the other members of the party to do what they can, within their capabilities, to contribute to the rescue effort. For example, some of the other good swimmers might swim out part of the way, in order to help pull their endangered comrade in to shore once he is brought within their reach. Others might prepare a vehicle to transport their friend to the nearest hospital, or else telephone the emergency services to send an ambulance. Expecting one member of the party to carry the full burden of the rescue, simply because he happens to be the best swimmer, seems manifestly unfair in this case.

So why should it be any different in the case of humanitarian intervention? This is clearly a significant problem, and one that remains unaddressed by Pattison's approach. It must be stressed, though, that it is not a problem particular to Pattison's framework, as it arises on any account in which a single intervener or coalition of interveners must act on the international community's responsibility to protect. I will not attempt to resolve this problem here but, as we shall see in the next chapter, being aware of it is important when considering the possibility of employing a contracted combatant force for humanitarian intervention.

Of course, a purely contracted combatant force has never been the primary instrument for undertaking a humanitarian intervention, and this situation is unlikely to arise in the near future. Nonetheless, there is significant heuristic value in asking whether there are any circumstances in which this might be a morally legitimate state of affairs. Providing an answer to that question is the task of the next chapter.

9 Contractors to the Rescue

I submit that the right to protect oneself from violations of one's own human rights by others is a human right, in the sense that it is a right to a freedom (to wit, the freedom to defend oneself, without interference, against others) which we need in order to lead a minimally flourishing life. By extension, the right to wage a war in defense of one's human rights should also be conceived of as a human right.

Cecile Fabre[1]

While brief and necessarily incomplete, the preceding chapter's summary of Pattison's moderate instrumentalist approach should suffice to enable us to assess how contracted combatants measure up on Pattison's scale. It must be stressed once more that we are here considering the hypothetical case of an intervention force made up entirely of contracted combatants. This is in fact a highly unlikely scenario – it is far more likely that an intervention involving contracted combatants will involve them as part of a broader coalition, or in support of a lead nation's state military forces.[2] The reason for focusing here on the unlikely scenario of a 'pure' contracted combatant intervention is that this is generally considered to be among the most morally fraught scenarios for the use of private warriors, and so allows us to consider the moral issues in their fullest form (even Pattison concedes that an intervention that involves contractors in a supporting role to traditional military forces might not be overly morally problematic, all things being equal).

CONTRACTED COMBATANTS AND LOCAL EXTERNAL EFFECTIVENESS

The primary and only necessary criterion for legitimate humanitarian intervention is the consequentialist consideration of the likely effectiveness of the intervention. Pattison contends that under sufficiently extreme circumstances an intervener who fulfils only one of the three criteria of effectiveness – local external effectiveness – and none of the other consequentialist or non-consequentialist criteria, might nonetheless be sufficiently legitimate to undertake the intervention.

The first and most obvious of the qualities necessary for effectiveness in a humanitarian intervention is the possession of the necessary military resources, including appropriately trained and motivated personnel, equipment such as vehicles and weapons, and strategic lift capability. None of these considerations represent a barrier to employing contractors for humanitarian interventions. If screening and selection mechanisms are rigorously applied then there is no reason in principle why appropriate personnel could not be found to take on the task at hand. As Mark Cancian has pointed out, contracted combatants employed in Iraq and Afghanistan have shown themselves to be, in general, 'highly professional'.[3] In fact, the private sector has a particular advantage over more traditional military forces when it comes to selecting personnel for humanitarian interventions. The military usually considers which of its formed units (battalions, brigades and the like) that are available are the best fit to the task at hand. Often, given other commitments, there is very little choice in the matter and the unit or units deployed may not be especially suited to the particularities of the operational environment. The private sector, on the other hand, recruits contractors for the specific mission being undertaken, which gives a significantly greater degree of flexibility and 'fit-to-purpose' in recruiting. For example, many of today's active private military/security companies draw a significant proportion of their personnel from former members of the law enforcement community. The UN, in contrast, is consistently unable to recruit sufficient police officers for its missions.[4]

Equipment and strategic lift capability are also not a problem. Very few states maintain significant 'in-house' equipment manufacture capabilities, and the vast majority of military equipment of all kinds is produced by, and available from, the private sector. Even warships can be leased from private companies. For example *HMS Clyde*, a River Class Offshore Patrol Vessel (Helicopter) armed with a 30mm gun and several smaller machine guns, is under lease from Vosper Thornycroft Shipbuilding by the Royal Navy and serves as the RN's Falkland Islands Patrol Vessel.[5] Likewise, while top-tier states do retain specialized strategic lift capabilities (such as the C-17 Globemaster III strategic/tactical airlifter operated by the Air Forces of the United States, Great Britain, Australia and Canada) not available on the open market, by far the bulk of strategic lift capability for military operations of a broadly humanitarian nature (such as the AU/UN mission in the Darfur region of Sudan) is provided by private sector logistical firms.

What of the requirement that, to be effective, an intervener must have the political and economic resources necessary to address the underlying causes of the conflict and help build stability? Because our hypothetical contracted combatant force will not be the intervener *per se*, but rather the agent of the intervener (either a state or a coalition of states), this criterion does not apply directly to the contracted combatant force. Put another way, the question of whether or not this criterion is met is independent of whether or not the force being employed is made up of contracted combatants or traditional military personnel.

Other direct qualities of an effective intervener include the intervener having an appropriate strategy for achieving the goals of the intervention, and the political will to make full use of the resources available for the intervention. In one respect these qualities are similar to those I have just addressed – they are largely independent of the issue of which type of military force is deployed to undertake the mission at hand. Nonetheless, there are some points to be made here. First, it is worth noting that if the strategic planning for the mission is left in the hands of the contracted force, there is no reason in principle (if the potential for shirking is properly addressed, as outlined previously) why the strategy that emerges should be any less suitable for the mission than if it were drawn up by state military planners. Indeed, in the US in particular, the military depends heavily on contractors from firms like MPRI to run simulations, exercises and help prepare campaign plans.

Secondly, while political will is also in some sense independent of what type of military force is deployed for the humanitarian intervention, in that such an intervention will always be costly and difficult, there is nonetheless an argument to be made that an intervention can be successful with comparatively *less* political will if it is undertaken by a contracted force. As Hugh Smith points out in his study of 'casualty aversion' in recent military operations, 'When national interest is not deeply engaged, governments and citizens naturally prefer low-cost, low-risk operations.'[6] A contracted force can help in both respects. Firstly, while it is not a given, there is good reason to think that a force of contracted combatants can do the job at a lower long-term cost. A recent study by the United States' Congressional Budget Office which considered the costs of replacing the contractors supporting US forces in Iraq and Afghanistan with military units concluded that, 'over the long term, using military units would cost 90 percent more than using contractors, and would have high upfront costs associated with equipping the new units'.[7] Risk, at least the kind of risk that tends to affect political will (in particular, the risk of casualties among national troops), is also reduced by the employ-ment of a contracted combatant force. Note that here I am not focusing on the question of whether or not this pervasive fact about political will is or is not morally appropriate (I will return to this question shortly), but only its impact on the likelihood of the intervention being effective.

Proximity is singled out by Pattison as being important because of the increased likelihood that the intervener will have an adequate degree of understanding of the culture or cultures in the geographic locale into which the intervention is to take place, and because countries that are proximate to the region being destabilized by the human rights violations which the intervention is intended to address are likely to have a vested interest in seeing the situation stabilized as quickly and effectively as possible. The issue of vested interest has more to do with the country backing the intervention than it has to do with which forces (state military or private military) it chooses to employ to undertake the intervention. Regarding cultural understanding, however, private military companies offer a significant advantage over state military forces. For one thing, economic considerations generally push these companies to employ local personnel wherever possible (it is often forgotten, for example, that the vast majority of armed contractors in Iraq are Iraqi nationals), with a consequent gain in local knowledge as well as a reduction in the intervention's overall 'footprint' in the local cultural environment. Furthermore, because contracted combatants and other contractors are recruited for specific operations rather than being a standing force, there is far greater opportunity to recruit personnel with relevant cultural and language skills. There are therefore real opportunities here to avoid some of the problems caused by, as the character Osmon Atto put it in the film *Black Hawk Down* (2001), sending 'a bunch of Arkansas white boys' to somewhere as culturally alien to them as, say, Somalia.

Another consideration singled out by Pattison as a likely feature of an effective intervener is that of responsiveness. It must be conceded here that there exist state-based military forces that are likely to be able to respond to a crisis more rapidly than a force of contracted combatants could be assembled and deployed. The NATO Rapid Response Force, for example, is designed to be able to begin deployment after five days notice, and consists of a force of up to 15,000 troops.[8] Likewise, the emerging African

Union Standby Brigades, when fully operational, are expected to provide a rapid response capability for Africa. The fact remains, however, that since its inception the NATO Rapid Response Force has not been employed for humanitarian intervention operations, and there are significant doubts as to whether the AU Standby Brigades will ever be used for this purpose, given the myriad political and legal obstacles to their employment.[9] A far more common trend is for state-based forces to take a very long time to deploy for operations that are not in the urgent national interest, a problem exacerbated by the fact that most troop-contributing nations are from the developing world. African security expert Henri Boshoff, for example, wrote in 2007 that 'African nations have a dismal history of failing to make good on offers of personnel and resources. The AU has missed every deployment deadline for force enhancement in Darfur since first deploying in summer 2004.'[10] This is a common lament, and against this background it is difficult to dispute the claim regularly made by supporters of the private military/security industry that contracted combatants can in many cases do the job 'faster, better, cheaper'.

CONTRACTED COMBATANTS AND GLOBAL EXTERNAL EFFECTIVENESS

Thus far we have considered what Pattison calls 'local external effectiveness', that is, the likely effectiveness of the intervener in combating the massive violations of basic human rights that give rise to the need for the intervention in the first place. A hypothetical force of contracted combatants appears to fare well in this regard. But there are two additional aspects of effectiveness to be considered, namely global external effectiveness and internal effectiveness. Global external effectiveness seems generally unlikely to be affected differently by the intervener making use of a contracted combatant force rather than a state military force. Still, there may be circumstances in which this will make

a difference. For example, there is a very negative view of contracted combatants among many African governments, due to a
perception that they are all cut from the same cloth as characters
like 'Black' Jack Schramme, 'Mad' Mike Hoare and others who
ran amok on African soil in the middle decades of the twentieth
century. While it is hard to imagine how this sort of sensitivity
might lead to circumstances in which an intervention composed
of a contracted combatant force would result in regional instability that would further threaten the enjoyment of basic human
rights, this is a question that must nevertheless be asked in any
particular situation. More likely to be an issue is the *indirect* effect
of employing the contracted combatant force on the overall
effectiveness of the intervention. Perceived legitimacy is sometimes a factor in the success of the intervention (though not
always, as in the case of NATO's illegal intervention in Kosovo),
and the use of a contracted combatant force might, depending
on the prevailing outlook on the use of such forces, potentially be
an obstacle to effectiveness. The degree to which that is the case
must be measured against the other factors that are indicative of
effectiveness.

CONTRACTED COMBATANTS AND INTERNAL EFFECTIVENESS

Far clearer is the likely impact that employing a contracted
combatant force for an intervention will have on internal effectiveness. If, as many have argued, it is true that a contracted combatant force would represent a less costly means of undertaking
an intervention, then such a force is, relative to the financial
saving involved, less likely to lead to a reduction in the enjoyment
of basic human rights by the citizens of the country or countries
undertaking the intervention (caused by, for example, poverty).
Furthermore, given that a contracted combatant force need not
consist entirely of citizens of the country or countries funding

the intervention, it is also likely to result in proportionally fewer citizen deaths among those engaged in the intervention than would be the case with an equivalent state military force. An additional relevant consideration here is the challenge of recruitment. Western military forces like the US and the UK have in recent years struggled to meet recruiting targets (though the current economic downturn seems to be having a positive effect in this regard). As the renowned British military historian Sir Michael Howard once rather pointedly pointed out, 'The flower of British and French manhood had not flocked to the colours in 1914 to die for the balance of power.'[11] The same challenge of motivation lies behind the difficulty in recruiting Western soldiers to serve in operations in places like Iraq and Afghanistan which, while not humanitarian interventions themselves, reflect many of the challenges and complexities of that kind of military adventure. The same, however, cannot be said for the private sector – there have been no shortage of experienced and professional men and women taking up contracts in support of those very same operations.

Though the consequentialist considerations discussed above are key features of a legitimate intervener, a pure consequentialist approach would be in danger of leading to unhappy excesses. For this reason Pattison adds three non-consequentialist criteria of legitimacy, namely: adherence to *jus in bello* norms, internal representativeness, and external local representativeness. How does our hypothetical contracted combatant force fare when considered against these measures?

CONTRACTED COMBATANTS AND *JUS IN BELLO*

One of Pattison's main concerns about the employment of contracted combatants is that the lack of appropriate mechanisms (legal and otherwise) by which to control such forces leads to a danger that making use of a contracted combatant force could lead to violations of 'external' *jus in bello* norms (the traditional norms guiding the intervener's treatment of civilians and enemy combatants). But, as argued in Chapter 7, even if Pattison's concerns are currently justified, there is no reason why such controls cannot be put in place, and so there are no reasons why we should think that a contracted combatant force must *necessarily* pose such a risk.

The internal principles of *jus in bello* that Pattison singles out are the requirements that the intervener employ only appropriate combatants in undertaking the intervention, and that the intervener fulfil a duty of care towards the combatants deployed on humanitarian interventions. I have already acknowledged Pattison's concern that states may fail to fulfil the latter duty in the case of contracted combatants, but this is not an intrinsic feature of the employment of contracted combatants, and we might hope that greater awareness will lead to this becoming less of a problem in the future.

It is the requirement of employing only appropriate combatants for humanitarian interventions that is of most interest here. By singling out child soldiers and conscripts as inappropriate for such missions, Pattison raises the key issue of *consent*. Martin Cook writes that:

> Military personnel live in a unique world. They exist to serve the state. The essence and moral core of their service is to defend that state through the management and application of violence in defense of the territorial integrity, political sovereignty, and vital national interests of that state. Their contract has an 'unlimited liability' clause – they accept (and in an all-volunteer force, unquestionably voluntarily accept) the obligation to put their lives and bodies at grave risk when ordered to do so. Their contract also requires them to kill other human beings and to destroy their property when given legal orders to do so.[12]

A question arises, however, as to whether the obligation to risk death and injury continues to hold in cases where the defence of

the state or its vital interests is not at stake, as we might think is
often the case in humanitarian interventions (though, obviously,
this issue is avoided in cases where the intervention is undertaken for reasons of national interest). It is far from obvious that
the obligation 'transfers' to the international community or its
representatives (for example the UN or regional organizations).[13]
There is, furthermore, according to Olsthoorn, reason to question whether societal change in the West and with it a reluctance
to make sacrifices, makes it 'probably a bit too optimistic . . . to
think that the global village will be the kind of community we are
willing to make sacrifices for'.[14]

The core moral challenge here is well articulated by Michael
Gross who writes,

> If humanitarian intervention imposes a duty on democratic states
> that they *'owe* to victims of internal crises and crimes' as Stanley
> Hoffmann demands, then someone, namely the soldiers of the state
> that intervenes, must bear the cost of protecting other human beings
> from genocide, enslavement, ethnic cleansing and wanton rape and
> murder. These costs are not trivial because some soldiers will die.
> But unless we are prepared to assume them, humanitarian interven-
> tion will fail. . . . Here we face what John Lango has called the 'moral
> paradox' of humanitarian intervention: 'even if it is obligatory for a
> state (collectively) to intervene, it can still be supererogatory (indi-
> vidually) for its citizens'. Low costs, great benefits and the prospect of
> relatively few casualties obligate the state to intercede. High costs and
> the prospect of death, on the other hand, release each citizen from the
> very same duty.[15]

While Pattison concedes some of the weight of this argument, he
doubts that it is truly a debilitating paradox, as Gross suggests.
Pattison argues that while it might be true that the primary moral
obligation of the soldier, sailor, airman or marine is to his or her
state, the idea that humanitarian interventions are not the sort
of missions that these individuals 'signed up for' cannot stand in
the face of the fact that this kind of mission has become one of

the primary purposes for which armed forces have been used in recent decades. Consequently, contends Pattison, anyone who volunteers for military service must, therefore, be aware that in so doing he is consenting to the possibility that he will be required to serve in humanitarian interventions. And so the paradox is avoided. As Gross puts it:

> Volunteering replaces a state-imposed obligation with one that is self-imposed thereby allowing states to undertake humanitarian intervention without the worry of imposing undue risk on particular individuals. Just as police officers and fire-fighters voluntarily risk their lives to serve and protect other members of their community, volunteer humanitarian forces accept similar risks to defend citizens of foreign countries.[16]

What are the consequences of all this for assessing the ethics of employing contracted combatants for humanitarian interventions? Let us start by considering the implications if Gross is right and Pattison's response fails to defuse the 'moral paradox of humanitarian intervention'. (I'm inclined to believe that there is more to the paradox than is addressed by Pattison, but confess myself unable, at time of writing, to come up with good reasons to support this intuition.)[17] If the paradox holds, if Gross is correct that 'In the absence [of] vital military, national or strategic interests no state may risk the lives of its soldiers',[18] the same certainly cannot be said to be true of contracted combatants. Private warriors sign on for specific missions, and so there can be no question of their consenting to the specifics of the mission concerned, whether it be a humanitarian intervention or otherwise. It seems, therefore (if Gross is correct), that the employment of contracted combatants for humanitarian interventions provides a means whereby states can fulfil their moral obligations to intervene, without thereby violating their moral obligations to their military personnel.

What if Pattison is right? In that case, we can view modern soldiers, sailors, airmen and marines as, in effect, consenting to

a general requirement that they serve in humanitarian interventions. Even if this is so, it seems that employing contracted
combatants (in this regard at least) for actual humanitarian interventions must be considered to be morally preferable. For though
the individual solider, sailor, airman or marine may be understood
as consenting *in general* to undertake humanitarian interventions, the contracted combatant consents to risking his or her life
and limb in support of a *specific* humanitarian intervention. The
consent of the contracted combatant must, therefore, be considered to carry more moral weight.

Consider an analogy which will help illustrate this. Consent is
a critical element in the ethics of biomedical research. When new
drugs or medical procedures are tested on human subjects, their
consent is of the utmost importance. But consent is not given in a
general way – volunteers do not sign a generic consent form that
outlines in broad terms every potential consequence that they
might face from an array of possible and some as yet unimagined
medical interventions. Instead, the brave medical volunteer consents to submitting to the testing of a specific drug or medical
procedure on his or her body, and every effort is made to stipulate
as accurately as possible the potential effects, both negative and
positive, that the volunteer subject could experience. Clearly,
specific consent like this carries far more moral weight than the
broad consent to volunteer for 'medical research' (indeed, it is
doubtful whether the generic kind of consent would be considered sufficient to ensure the ethical standing of the research programme). Likewise, it seems clear that the specific consent of the
contracted combatant should carry more moral weight than the
general consent to participating in humanitarian interventions
that Pattison argues military personnel give. As a consequence,
contracted combatants must be deemed to better fulfil this
requirement of internal *jus in bello*.

CONTRACTED COMBATANTS AND INTERNAL REPRESENTATIVENESS

Internal representativeness will, in the first instance, be a question of the support for the intervention among the citizens of the country or countries undertaking the intervention, which is an issue independent of what type of force (whether contracted or state) is employed for the actual operation. That is not, however, to say that the issue of what kind of force is used is irrelevant here, as becomes apparent when we consider the reasons Pattison gives for giving internal representativeness the weight he does. The first reason is consequentialist, one of the indirect qualities of effectiveness that Pattison identifies. Simply put, an intervention that has the support of the citizens of the state or states undertaking the intervention has a greater likelihood of success, in that the political will to do what it takes to achieve the goals of the intervention is more likely to be in place. The second reason Pattison gives for taking internal representativeness seriously is what he calls the 'resources argument'. Here the idea is that, because the citizens of a country are also the taxpayers, the resources being invested in any proposed intervention are ultimately theirs, and the intervention should therefore reflect their will. Pattison points out that the resources provided by the citizens are both material and human. Finally, argues Pattison, the moral importance of individual self-government comes into play. Individual citizens ought to have a say in the running of their political institutions, and given the significance of a humanitarian intervention, the citizens' opinions matter. This is not simply because of the resource question, but also because the state represents its citizens when taking such actions.

There is a strong case here for the idea that employing contracted combatants will make meeting the requirement of internal representativeness easier to achieve. If that is true, then this is clearly a morally significant advantage that a contracted combatant force has over its state equivalent, for the easier it is to

meet the conditions for legitimate intervention (without weaken-
ing those conditions) the greater the likelihood is that there will
be potential interveners who could legitimately undertake the
intervention. Consider, firstly, the consequentialist consideration
outlined above. Political will is, of course, a fickle thing. While the
cost of a deployment might be an issue that threatens to undermine that political will, it is generally the more emotive issue of
the cost in human lives among the nation's military forces that
most quickly erodes political will. This is, for reasons we've already
covered, less likely to be the case with regard to casualties among
contracted combatants.

The material resources demanded of citizens (indirectly, via the
state) to enable a humanitarian intervention are, if the argument
for cost savings through contracting holds, comparatively lower
when contracted combatants are used for the mission. To that
degree, then, the challenge of securing internal representativeness for an intervention undertaken in this way is decreased.
Even more significant is the impact when human resources are
considered. For better or for worse, the 'cost' in terms of battlefield casualties weighs considerably less on contemporary
societies when those casualties are contracted combatants than
when they are soldiers, sailors, marines or airmen of the nation's
military services. This holds to an even greater degree when the
contracted combatants are citizens of nations other than the ones
undertaking the intervention.

At first glance this social reality seems to be a form of callous
chauvinism. Drawing this conclusion would, however, be too
quick, for there is another important consideration here, namely
the third factor that accounts for the importance of internal representativeness: individual self-governance. As mentioned above,
when a government, say that of Britain, sends troops from its
military services to undertake a humanitarian intervention, there
is an important sense in which those troops represent the people
of the United Kingdom of Great Britain and Northern Ireland. For
Britons those are *our* troops, they represent *us*. That identification

is, however, considerably loosened or even broken when those sent into the fray wear a different uniform or no uniform at all. There is ample evidence of this from recent experience: sticking with the British example, the British government is at the time of writing facing a considerable challenge in convincing the British people to continue to support the deployment of British troops in Afghanistan.

By contrast, the British government faces no such problems when it comes to contributing funds that are used to send UN peacekeepers from developing world nations into zones of conflict. Of course those troops are 'ours' for the people of some nation, so the problem is not entirely avoided. But what if UN member states funded a Security Council-approved humanitarian intervention that was conducted by one or more multinational private military companies? Again, it seems that in such a case the threshold for meeting the criterion of internal representativeness would be significantly lower, which represents a significant advantage where a contracted combatant force, rather than a state military force, is employed.

CONTRACTED COMBATANTS AND LOCAL EXTERNAL REPRESENTATIVENESS

Finally, following Pattison's 'moderate instrumentalist approach', there is the requirement of 'local external representativeness'. What impact is employing a contracted combatant force likely to have on the acceptance of the intervention by those who the intervention is designed to help, as well as affected bystanders? The answer will, of course, depend on the specific circumstances of the intervention. If the intervention is to take place in a country where a previous generation of contracted combatants has committed atrocities, then the likelihood is strong that a contracted combatant force will not be welcomed. It depends, also, on who is 'behind' the contracted combatant force. If, say, the United States is the employer of the force, and the US is very unpopular in that region, then it may make little difference that the troops on the ground are not uniformed US military personnel (though it is at least possible that judicious selection of personnel with appropriate cultural knowledge and backgrounds could ameliorate local hostility to some degree). On the other hand, there is also a case to be made that a contracted combatant force employed under a UN mandate and backed by a broad multinational coalition could be seen by local actors as apolitical, thereby reducing the potential for tensions between locals and the intervening force. It is also important to note that in circumstances severe enough to warrant a humanitarian intervention (such as genocide or ethnic cleansing), any effective intervener is likely to be welcomed by the affected community, regardless of their country of origin or contractual status. Certainly, the anecdotal evidence suggests that those citizens of Sierra Leone who were rescued by Executive Outcomes from the horrific slaughter and mutilations carried out by the RUF weren't particularly bothered by the fact that the EO personnel they welcomed as liberators were contracted combatants.

CONTRACTED COMBATANTS AND THE PROBLEM OF FAIRNESS

Before concluding this assessment of how a contracted combatant force fares when considered in the light of Pattison's framework for establishing the legitimacy of potential humanitarian interveners, it is important that we also consider the impact of the problem of fairness I outlined in the previous chapter. I argued that this problem arises when the general duty to intervene which falls on the international community at large must be carried out by a specific intervener, because the said intervener is adjudged to be the most legitimate. That the fact of legitimacy should thereby require the selected intervener to carry the human and economic burden of the intervention alone seems manifestly unfair. Employing a contracted combatant force for the intervention, however, offers a means to avoid this problem. For while it may be technically difficult to achieve, there is no reason in principle why every member of the United Nations could not be required to contribute financially in support of such an intervention force to the degree to which they can (without violating the principle of internal effectiveness) do so. Because the contracted combatant force is not the intervener *per se*, but only the tool of the intervener to which it is contracted, it becomes possible to meaningfully consider that such an arrangement will be a case of the international community conducting a humanitarian intervention. This would clearly be desirable, not least because it would ensure that the burden of the duty to intervene is fairly spread among the members of the international community.

CONCLUSION

Pattison wisely warns us not to attempt to determine legitimacy in the case of humanitarian intervention as a fixed variable – the legitimacy of an intervener will almost always depend on the circumstances of the particular intervention being proposed. That will be as true for the intervener which offers a force of contracted combatants as its intervening force as it is for interveners who propose to undertake the mission using state military forces. Nonetheless, it seems that, when measured against Pattison's comprehensive framework of analysis for determining the legitimacy of potential humanitarian interveners, our hypothetical contracted combatant force not only does not comprehensively fail to meet the criterion of the 'moderate instrumentalist account', but in fact in some respects fares better than an equivalent force composed of state military personnel. Furthermore, the employment of a contracted combatant force avoids a significant problem with humanitarian intervention, the problem of fairness. What is clear is that, at the conceptual level at least, the dismissive attitude of policy-makers and thinkers like Michael Walzer to the idea of employing contracted combatants for humanitarian interventions is unwarranted. This is an issue that should be considered on its merits for each specific instance of prospective humanitarian intervention, and it seems very possible that in some of those cases a contracted combatant force could well be found to meet the necessary criteria of legitimacy. In this regard Patricia Owens is to be applauded when she writes that, 'The meaningful comparison today is perhaps not "between private financing and/or delivery of security and the financing and/or delivery of security of states". It may be the different, albeit much more difficult to measure, contrast between expressions of force that increase global social and economic inequality and the likelihood of genocide, and those that do not.'[19]

Conclusion

*Lethal force is still a central determinant of international politics, and it is
simply ignoring reality to pretend otherwise . . .*

Nicholas Rennger and Caroline Kennedy-Pipe[1]

In a brace of very influential books, *The Shield of Achilles*[2] and
Terror and Consent,[3] Philip Bobbitt (Herbert Wechsler Professor of
Jurisprudence at Columbia University)[4] discusses the impact on
law and strategy of what he sees as an epochal change in international relations. Bobbitt argues that the demise of the Soviet
Union brought to an end what he calls the Long War,[5] the sum of
a long-running series of conflicts beginning with the First World
War. The Long War was in essence about which constitutional
order (National Socialism, Communism or parliamentary democracy) would become accepted as the legitimate constitutional
form for the nation state. Ironically, argues Bobbitt, the strategic
innovations that led to the victory of parliamentary democracy in
the battle for the soul of the nation state – particularly the development of weapons of mass destruction and global communications systems – also resulted in the beginning of the demise of the
nation state and the emergence of its successor, the market state.
Bobbitt explains as follows:

> Whereas the nation-state, with its mass free public education, univer-
> sal franchise, and social security policies, promised to guarantee the
> welfare of the nation, the market-state promises instead to maximize

the opportunity of the people and thus tends to privatize many state activities and to make voting and representative government less influential and more responsive to the market.[6]

Both strategy and law-making, Bobbitt argues, must take into account the new emerging environment of a world of market states. One of Bobbitt's observations about the market state is of particular relevance for this enquiry: 'The market-state does not so clearly demark the military from the commercial as did the nation-state.'[7] (Interestingly, Bobbitt made this observation in 2002, before the invasion of Iraq and the subsequent unprecedented boom in private military/security contracting. Bobbitt is not writing here with contracted combatants in mind, but is instead thinking of the All Volunteer Force, which he considers to be a product of market mechanisms.)

Whether or not we agree with Bobbitt on the emergence of market states, it would be difficult to resist the principle inherent in his admonition that 'Nostalgia aside . . . it is important to identify which cultural and political struggles are simply hangovers from the dying nation-state and its resistance to the form of the new market-state and which are genuine choices that the market-state brings to life.'[8] We need to ask ourselves how much of the resistance to the employment of contracted combatants that we are seeing in today's media and academic circles is the product of nostalgia for a past era rather than the product of rigorous analysis?

A proper answer to that (to which this book is only a preliminary and partial response) should decide the question of whether or not society ought to recognize the contracted combatant as a legitimate professional (a question I left hanging in Chapter 3). Drawing on Andrew Abbott's work on professions, Martin Cook points out that a profession's legitimacy 'is not a fixed, immutable fact. Rather, professions jockey for positions within a given society as different professions and non-professional groups attempt to gain jurisdiction over spheres of human labour that previously have belonged to other professional groups, or, alternatively, as professions attempt to protect their historical jurisdiction from encroachments by competitor professions.'9 This seems precisely the sort of dynamic that we observe today between the military, and the private military industry. What the outcome of this process will be remains to be seen. Will the contracted combatant eventually be seen as a fully fledged military professional, on a par with the soldiers, sailors, marines and airmen of a nation's armed forces? Or will contracted combatants come to be seen as members of a kind of supporting profession, like the nursing profession or the emerging paralegal profession?10

I have argued in this book that the contracted combatant is just (merely, simply) a warrior, and the conditions that determine whether or not individual contracted combatants can be considered Just (moral, ethical) warriors are essentially the same as those that must be considered when asking the same question of state military personnel. David Isenberg is largely correct that, 'The legitimate concerns about the legal and ethical role and status of private military contractors flow from the fact that international law has not kept pace with the changing nature of war and PMCs.'11 But this is simply a contingent fact about the legal arrangements that happen to apply in the current international environment – there is no *intrinsic* reason why we should reject the employment of contracted combatants. It is hard to find fault with economist Jürgen Brauer's claim that 'The make-or-buy decision, i.e., to what degree to produce force in-house by the nation-state or to out-source its production is entirely analogous to make-or-buy decisions of modern private households (do-it-yourself or hire a plumber) and firms (maintain a human resources department or hire via a personnel agency). The make-or-buy decision itself is utterly irrelevant. What is relevant is who makes the decision, under whose authority and for what ultimate purpose . . .'.12

Doubtless this kind of stark economic language will cause

discomfort for many readers, and feed concerns that this kind of thinking reflects a troubling shift from what Bobbit calls a 'democratic political matrix' to a 'capitalist market matrix'.

> But this would mistake the way we deal with problems for the problems themselves: there will always be a political and a market mechanism working in tandem because the kind of problems states must solve cannot be wholly assimilated into one or the other approach. . . . One can never be wholly sacrificed to the other in a civilized society. Indeed one might go so far as to say that it is a distinguishing mark of a civilized society that it struggles to maintain many-valued forms of life despite the human condition of scarcity that compels choice among these forms.[13]

Among the values that should not be sacrificed in a civilized society is the idea that warriors are to be honoured by those they serve, and should never be treated as mere means to some end. If the state's use of contracted combatants is to be legitimate, then Shannon French's eloquent words about warriors in general must be applied to the private warrior too:

> Warriors are not mere tools; they are complex, sentient beings with fears, loves, hopes, dreams, talents, and ambitions – all of which may soon be snuffed out by a bomb, bullet, or bayonet. . . . [T]hose who send them off to war must make an effort to ensure that the warriors themselves fully understand the purpose of, and need for, their sacrifice. Those heading into harm's way must be given sincere assurances that their lives will not be squandered, and their leaders must not betray their trust. . . . [T]he state must show concern for what will happen to its warriors after the battles are won (or lost). The dead should be given decent burials (if it is possible) and appropriate memorials. Those wounded in body should be given the best medical care, and treatment should be made available for those with psychological wounds. Former warriors must be welcomed back into the communities that spawned them and sent them away to do what needed to be done.[14]

If there is one aspect in which the current debate has tended to miss the point about contracted combatants, it is in its focus on the contractors themselves rather than on the states that employ them. But, as I have tried to show here, the really important ethical issues come down to the responsibility of the state for its decisions about the exercise of armed force and the agents that exercise force on its behalf. David Isenberg is again right in saying the key issue here is that 'states bear responsibility for the actions of contractors they employ', and this is a responsibility that they ought not to be allowed to evade.[15] Ensuring this will require legal and other mechanisms to be put in place, and a system of dealing with contracted combatants which rises above the merely ad hoc and contingency quality of most current arrangements. Mark Cancian makes the useful suggestion that the recent evolution in the role and employment of reservists offers a helpful analogy for the evolution which should be taking place in addressing the employment of contractors.[16]

A question that I have not attempted to address here, but one that will certainly need to be addressed in the literature on the private provision of armed force, is whether or not it might ever be legitimate for an individual or a private entity like a corporation to employ contracted combatants to engage in warfighting. Certainly private contractors provide robust security services to private corporations in places like Nigeria's oil-rich Niger Delta, and at times this kind of security can be difficult to distinguish from combat, particularly in the face of determined insurgents. The idea that private citizens might have the right to wage war is not, as Cecile Fabre points out, a new one. The great sixteenth-century jurist Francisco de Vitoria, considered by many to be the 'father' of international law, claimed that 'any person, even a private citizen, may declare and wage a defensive war', and the equally eminent seventeenth-century jurist Hugo Grotius 'is quite clear in *The rights of war and peace* that a private man may wage war against his own state if no legal recourse is available . . ., as well as against a sovereign other than his own. . .'.[17] Fabre argues that a cosmopolitan account of Just War Theory must reject the traditional view of legitimate authority and instead accept as legitimate any individual or body that can be successfully defended 'by appealing to their ability to protect and promote human rights'.[18]

Whatever the merits of Fabre's argument, it alerts us to the fact that there is much that I have not covered in this book, which remains to be addressed in considering the ethics of employing contracted combatants. Indeed, there is no doubt much that remains to be said about what I *have* addressed in this book. I am not so naïve as to think that what I have offered could even begin to be considered the final word o.n this important topic. My hope, instead, is that the publication of this volume will stimulate more capable scholars than I to address this issue in a manner that considers contracted combatants on their merits, rather than through a filter of nostalgia and distrust. Fairness requires no less than that.

Introduction

1 Cancian, 2008, 'Contractors: The New Element of Military Force Structure', *Parameters*, Autumn, p. 61.

2 Peter W. Singer, 'Warriors for Hire in Iraq', *Salon.com*, 15 April, 2004. www.brookings.edu/articles/2004/0415defenseindustry_singer.aspx (Accessed 23 July 2009).

3 Cancian, op cit., p. 62.

4 ibid., p. 65.

5 Blackwater was renamed Xe in 2009.

6 Jeremy Scahill, 2007, *Blackwater: The Rise of the World's Most Powerful Mercenary Army* (1st edn), New York: Nation Books.

7 Named for the title of the Oscar-winning 2001 film *Black Hawk Down* and the book of the same title on which the movie was based (Mark Bowden, 1999, *Black Hawk Down: A Story of Modern War*, Berkeley, CA: Atlantic Monthly Press).

8 The case against the Blackwater contractors involved in this incident was dismissed by a US Federal judge in late December 2009. ('US judge dismisses charges in Blackwater Iraq Killings', BBC News Online http://news.bbc.co.uk/2/hi/americas/8436780.stm. Accessed 19 January 2010.)

9 Cancian, op. cit., p. 72. As Cancian points out, 'A small but vocal group advocates replacing civilian contractors with military personnel. This is not feasible. Replacing the 113,000 contractors in the security and logistics arenas (excluding interpreters and all those in reconstruction) would require a minimum of 250,000 additional military personnel, and when the rotation base and training pipeline

are considered the number quickly swells to more than 400,000 as a high-end estimate. With the Army struggling to meet the more modest target of its current expansion, an increase of 65,000 active-duty soldiers, such a large expansion would appear impossible without reconstituting the draft. Since a draft is opposed by the military leadership, politicians, and the American people as a whole, reinstituting conscription is infeasible, whatever its attraction for op-ed writers.' (Ibid.).

10 Cancian, op. cit., p. 65.
11 Ibid.
12 'Blackwater USA says it can supply forces for conflicts' http://content.hamptonroads.com/story.cfm?story=102251&ran=202519&tref=po. Accessed 17 July 2007.
13 Executive Outcomes founder, Eeben Barlow, has written a history of the organization entitled *Executive Outcomes: Against all Odds* (Galago Press, 2007).
14 Mervyn Frost, 2008, 'Regulating anarchy: The ethics of PMCs in global civil society', in Andrew Alexandra, Deane-Peter Baker and Marina Caparini (eds), *Private Military and Security Companies: Ethics, Policies and Civil–Military Relations*, London and New York,: Routledge, p. 54.
15 Patricia Owens, 2008, 'Distinctions, distinctions: "public" and "private" force?', *International Affairs*, **84**(5), p. 977.
16 See for example Doug Brooks and Matan Chorev, 'Ruthless humanitarianism: why marignalizing private peacekeeping kills people', in Andrew Alexandra, Deane-Peter Baker and Marina Caparini (eds) *Private Military and Security Companies: Ethics, Policies and Civil–Military Relations*, London and New York: Routledge, pp. 116–30.
17 C. A. J. Coady, 1992, 'Mercenary Morality', in *International Law and Armed Conflict*, A. G. D. Bradney (ed.), Stuttgart: Steiner, pp. 55–69. Coady takes a position that is, broadly speaking, negative about the moral standing of 'mercenaries'.
18 Asa Kasher, 2008, 'Interface Ethics: Military Forces and Private Military Companies' in Andrew Alexandra, Deane-Peter Baker, and Marina Caparini (eds), *Private Military and Security Companies: Ethics, Policies and Civil-Military Relations*, London and New York: Routledge, pp. 235–46.

Chapter 1

1 Originally published in David Grossman, 2004, *On Combat: The psychology and physiology of deadly conflict in war and peace*, PPCT Research Publications. Excerpted here from www.killology.com/sheep_dog.htm (accessed 28 October 2008).

2 Martin Cook, 2004, *The Moral Warrior: Ethics and Service in the U.S. Military*, New York: State University of New York Press, p. 21.

3 Shannon E. French, 2003, *The Code of the Warrior: Exploring Warrior Values Past and Present*, New York: Rowman and Littlefield, p. 3.

4 Quoted in James Toner, 1995, *True Faith and Allegiance: The Burden of Military Ethics*, Lexington, KY: University of Kentucky Press, p. 20.

5 This account is drawn from Lt Murphy's Medal of Honor citation (www.navy.mil/moh/mpmurphy/oc.html, accessed 14 April 2009) and the article 'Highest Honor for Afghan War Hero' by April Drew (17 October 2007, *Irish Voice News*, www.irishabroad.com/news/irish-voice/news/afghan-war-hero171007.aspx (accessed 14 April 2009).

6 William Ian Miller, *The Mystery of Courage*, Cambridge, MA; Harvard University Press, 2000, p. 47.

7 Peter Olsthoorn, 2007, 'Courage in the Military: Physical and Moral' in *Journal of Military Ethics*, **6**(4), p. 270.

8 Peter Olsthoorn, 2005, 'Honor as a Motive for Making Sacrifices', *Journal of Military Ethics*, **4**(3), p. 183.

9 Plato, *Laches*. 191d–e.

10 Olsthoorn, 2007, p. 271.

11 Ibid., p. 274.

12 Interestingly, Lt Murphy's official Medal of Honor citation makes no mention of his morally courageous choice not to kill the goat herder, instead focusing on his physically courageous act of exposing himself to enemy fire in order to secure help for his comrades.

13 Toner, 1995, p. 117.

14 As Paul Robinson wryly puts it, 'Autonomous thinking, it seems, is only a virtue until it leads to conclusions which the military doesn't like.' (Robinson, 2007, 'Magnanimity and Integrity as Military Virtues', in *Journal of Military Ethics*, **6**(4), p. 263.)

15 Ibid., p. 263.

16 See Olsthoorn, 2005, p. 184.

17 Christopher Coker, 2001, *Humane Warfare*, London: Routledge.

18 See Christopher Coker, 2004, *The Future of War*, London: Wiley Blackwell.

19 Alasdair MacIntyre's *After Virtue: A Study in Moral Theory* (University of Notre Dame Press, 1981) is perhaps the most famous work to expound this view.

20 From William Manchester, *Goodbye, Darkness: A Memoir of the Pacific War*, quoted in French, 2003, p. 12.

21 William Shakespeare, *Henry V*, Act 4, Scene 3.

22 Olsthoorn, 2007, p. 257.

23 MacCoun, R., Kier, E. and Belkin, A., 2006, 'Does social cohesion determine motivation in combat? An old question with an old answer', *Armed Forces and Society*, **32**, p. 647, quoted in Olsthoorn 2007, p. 276.

24 Quoted in Toner, 1995, pp. 56–7.

25 Quoted in ibid., p. 121.

26 J. G. Peristiany (ed.), 1968, *Honour and Shame: The Values of Mediterranean Society*, London: Weidenfeld and Nicolson, p. 21.

27 See Paul Robinson's helpful discussion of magnanimity in Robinson 2007.

28 Quoted in Olsthoorn, 2005, p. 187.

29 Quentin Skinner, 1978, *The Foundations of Modern Political Thought: Vol. 1, The Rennaissance*, Cambridge: Cambridge University Press, p. 101.

30 *An Enquiry into the Origin of Honour, and the Usefulness of Christianity in War*, quoted in Olsthoorn, 2005, p. 188.

31 Olsthoorn, 2005, p. 186.

32 Moskos, Charles, Jr., 1986, 'Institutional/Occupational Trends in Armed Forces: An Update', *Armed Forces and Society*, **12**, pp. 377–82.

33 Robinson, 2007, p. 261.

34 Coker, 2004, p. 10.

35 French, 2003, p. 16.

36 Michael Ignatieff, 1998, *The Warrior's Honour: Ethnic War and the Modern Conscience*, Holt Paperbacks, p. 117.

37 Robinson, 2007, p. 264.

38 The story is recounted in Mark Osiel's *Obeying Orders: Atrocity,*

Military Discipline, and the Law of War (Transaction Publishers, 2001) and quoted in French 2003, p. 14.

39 Dan Baum, 'Battle Lessons, What the Generals Don't Know', *The New Yorker*, 17 January 2005, quoted in the U.S. Army/Marine Corps Counterinsurgency Field Manual, p. 241.

40 Cook, 2004, p. 74.

41 Coker, 2004, p. 6.

42 McCain in French, 2003, pp. x–xi.

43 Elke Krahmann, 2008, 'The new model soldier and civil–military relations' in Andrew Alexandra, Deane-Peter Baker and Marina Caparini (eds), *Private Military and Security Companies: Ethics, Policies and Civil–Military Relations* (New York: Routledge), p. 252.

44 See the discussion in ibid., p. 252ff.

45 Cook, op. cit., p. 62.

46 Krahmann, 2008, p. 253.

47 Cook, op. cit., p. 73.

48 Ibid., p. 67.

Chapter 2

1 www.flyingtigersavg.com/tiger1.htm (accessed 15 April 2009).

2 I don't address the 'dogs of war' label here, simply because I cannot think of any possible way in which this would usefully point to some identifiable moral failing in the private warrior. The term came to be associated with mercenaries as a result of Frederick Forsyth's 1974 novel of that title, but its use in this way seems to misrepresent the sense of the original use of the phrase in Scene 1, Act III of Shakespeare's *Julius Caesar* ('Cry Havoc, and let slip the dogs of war!'), which uses the word 'dogs' to refer to restraining mechanisms or latches, rather than to canines as is generally thought. I am grateful to Conway Waddington for pointing this out to me.

3 Patricia Owens, 2008, 'Distinctions, Distinctions: "Public" and "Private" Force?', *International Affairs*, **84**(5), p. 983. The quote is from Sarah Percy, *Mercenaries: the history of a norm in International Relations* (Oxford: Oxford University Press, 2007), p. 122.

4   For example, the *1977 Organisation of African Unity's Convention on the Elimination of Mercenarism in Africa*, one of the few legal 'anti-mercenary' instruments in international law, is a notoriously ineffective piece of legislation (see for example Sabelo Gumedze's analysis in his 'Towards the revision of the *1977 OAU/AU Convention on the Elimination of Mercenarism in Africa*', *African Security Review* **16**(4), pp. 22–33). It is sometimes said that anyone convicted on charges of mercenarism deserves to be shot, along with their lawyer!

5   Quoted in Uwe Steinhoff, 2008, 'What are mercenaries?' in Andrew Alexandra, Deane-Peter Baker and Marina Caparini (eds), *Private Military and Security Companies: Ethics, Policies and Civil–Military Relations* (New York: Routledge), pp. 19–20.

6   Ibid., p. 28.

7   Ibid., p. 21.

8   Ibid., p. 22.

9   In September 1990 the US Postal Service issued a 40 cent stamp honouring Claire Chennault.

10 Pamela Feltus (n.d.), 'Claire Chennault and the Flying Tigers of World War II', www.centennialofflight.gov/essay/Air_Power/tigers/AP24.htm (accessed 15 April 2009).

11 C. A. J. Coady, 1992, 'Mercenary Morality' in *International Law and Armed Conflict*, A. G. D. Bradney (ed.), Stuttgart: Steiner, pp. 55–69; Adrian Walsh and Tony Lynch, 2000, 'The Good Mercenary?', *Journal of Political Philosophy*, **8**(2), pp. 133–53.

12 Cancian, 2008, p. 71.

13 See Thomas More, 1974, 'Of Warfare' in *Utopia: A Dialogue of Comfort*, London: Heron Books, pp. 107–17.

14 Heidi L. Maibom and Fred Bennett, 2009, 'Patriotic Virtue', *Political Studies*, **57**, p. 655.

15 Coady, 1992, p. 62.

16 Patrick J. McGowan, 2003, 'African military coups d'état, 1956–2001: frequency, trends and distribution', *The Journal of Modern African Studies*, **41**(3), pp. 339–70.

17 James Pattison, 2008, 'Just War Theory and the Privatization of Military Force', *Ethics & International Affairs*, **22**(2), p. 146.

18 Lynch and Walsh, 2000, p. 136.

19 Pattison, 2008, p. 146.

20 Lynch and Walsh, op. cit., p. 136.

21 Ibid., 2000, p. 138.

22 Pattison, op. cit., 145–6.

23 Cécile Fabre, 'In Defence of Mercenarism', *British Journal of Political Science*, forthcoming 2010, www.cecilefabre.com/In%20Defence%20 of%20Mercenarism%20BJPS%20Final%20Draft.pdf (accessed 10 November 2009).

24 Fabre, op. cit.

25 Lynch and Walsh, op. cit., p. 138.

26 Fabre, op. cit.

27 Pattison, op. cit., p. 147.

28 Ibid., pp. 147–8.

29 Cited by Aquinas in 'Reply to Faoustus', XXII, 74, quoted in Anthony Coates, 'Culture, the Enemy and the Moral Restraint of War' in *The Ethics of War: Shared Problems in Different Traditions* (Richard Sorabji and David Rodin (eds), 2006, Aldershot: Ashgate, p. 216).

30 Lynch and Walsh, op. cit., p. 140.

31 Ibid., p. 140.

32 In a private communication Peter Baker has pointed out to me that it's noteworthy that contracted combatants are never referred to as 'prostitutes of war' but only ever 'whores of war'. He speculates that this might perhaps be because of a connotation of lustfulness and irresponsibility that is associated with the term 'whore' that is not necessarily associated with the term 'prostitute' (think, for example, of the idea of a 'high class' prostitute). Baker suggests that perhaps the core of analogy then is the concern that the mercenary has bloodlust or behaves in an uncontrollable or unruly way. This may indeed be true, but if it is it remains an unconvincing analogy. As I have argued earlier in this chapter, there is no particular reason to think that a contracted combatant will by definition be a psychotic killer. I address the issue of 'command and control' in Chapter 7.

33 Lars Ericsson, 1980, 'Charges against Prostitution: An Attempt at a Philosophical Assessment', *Ethics*, **90**, p. 33.

34 Carole Pateman, 1983, 'Defending Prostitution: Charges Against Ericcson', *Ethics*, **93**, p. 561.

35 See, for example, Scott Anderson, 2002, 'Prostitution and sexual autonomy: Making sense of the prohibition of prostitution', *Ethics*, **112**(4), pp. 748–80.
36 Fabre, op. cit.
37 Ibid.
38 Leviticus 21:9.
39 See, for example, Ezekiel 16.
40 This is a case of the formal fallacy of denying the antecedent. The structure of this fallacy is as follows:

> If *P*, then *Q*.
> Not *P*.
> Therefore, not *Q*.

The same structure is clearly evident in the argument that we are here considering:

> If a person is a citizen of country X, it is morally right that he should fight in defence of country X.
> A mercenary seeking to fight for country X would not be a citizen of country X.
> Therefore, it is not morally right that the mercenary should fight in defence of country X.

41 Lynch and Walsh, op. cit., p. 134.

Chapter 3

1 Sarah Percy, 2008, *Mercenaries: The History of a Norm in International Relations*, Oxford: Oxford University Press, abstract to Chapter 7, www.oxfordscholarship.com/oso/public/content/politicalscience/9780199214334/acprof-9780199214334-chapter-8.html (accessed 11 November 2009).
2 Attributed.
3 www.royalhumanesociety.org.uk/html/about.html (accessed 29 July 2009).
4 www.royalhumanesociety.org.uk/html/silver_medal.html (accessed 29 July 2009).
5 www.royalhumanesociety.org.uk/html/award_winners.html (accessed 29 July 2009).

6 Scahill, 2007, pp. 117–32.

7 Dana Priest, 'Private Guards Repel Attack on U.S. Headquarters', *Washington Post*, 6 April 2004 www.washingtonpost.com/ac2/wp-dyn?pagename=article&contentId=A53059-2004Apr5&notFound=true (accessed 30 July 2009).

8 Kim Curtis, 'Blackwater copter rescues Polish ambassador', The Associated Press, http://seattletimes.nwsource.com/html/nation-world/2003922642_webiraq03.html (accessed 30 July 2009).

9 Bernd Debusmann, 'In outsourced U.S. wars, contractor deaths top 1,000', Reuters, Tuesday, 3 July 2007, www.reuters.com/article/topNews/idUSN0318650320070703, (accessed 28 July 2009).

10 J. J. Messner, 2007, 'Credit Where Credit Is Due', *Journal of International Peace Operations*, **3**(3), (JIPO 3 v 3 Nov–Dec 2007), accessed at http://peaceops.com/web/v3n3/12-v3n3/115-v3n3creditewherecreditis-due.html (accessed 28 July 2009).

11 Telephone interview with ArmorGroup Chief Administrative Officer Christopher Beese, 24 July 2009.

12 Morten Hvaal, 'Another Road to Hell', *The Digital Journalist*, January 2007, issue 111. www.digitaljournalist.org/issue0701/another-road-to-hell.html (accessed 29 July 2009).

13 Associated Press, 'No forensic match for ammo in Blackwater shoot-ing', 1 April 2009 (www.usatoday.com/news/washington/2009-04-01-blackwater-report_N.htm, (accessed 30 July 2009). Some reports use the spelling 'Nisour'.

14 Voice of America News, 4 March 2007, 'US Revises Downward Number of Civilians Killed in Afghan Convoy Attack', www.voanews.com/english/archive/2007-03/2007-03-04-voa5.cfm?CFID=2609182 48&CFTOKEN=77062565&jsessionid=84305954fab6f51eb2a6366b6 e24155353a4 (accessed 30 July 2009).

15 Tim McGirk, 'Collateral Damage or Civilian Massacre in Haditha?', *Time*, 19 March 2006, www.time.com/time/world/article/0,8599, 1174649,00.html (accessed 20 July 2009).

16 David Isenberg, 2009, 'Private Military Contractors and U.S. Grand Strategy', *PRIO Report*. Oslo: PRIO, p. 12, www.prio.no/Research-and-Publications/Publication/?oid=49870671 (accessed 11 November 2009).

17 T. Christian Miller, 'U.S. Marines Detained 19 Contractors in Iraq', *Los*

Angeles Times, 8 June 2005, http://articles.latimes.com/2005/jun/08/world/fg-security8 (accessed 3 August 2009).

18 Ernesto Londoño, 'After the Shooting, Another Showdown', *Washington Post*, Saturday, 25 July 2009, www.washingtonpost.com/wp-dyn/content/article/2009/07/24/AR2009072403877.html?hpid=topnews (accessed 3 August 2009).

19 Telephone interview with ArmorGroup Chief Administrative Officer Christopher Beese, ArmorGroup, 24 July 2009.

20 Messner, 2007.

21 Telephone interview with ArmorGroup Chief Administrative Officer Christopher Beese, 24 July 2009.

22 Joseph Runzo, 2008, 'Benevolence, honourable soldiers and private military companies: Reformulating Just War theory' in Andrew Alexandra, Deane-Peter Baker and Marina Caparini (eds) *Private Military and Security Companies: Ethics, Policies and Civil–Military Relations*, New York: Routledge), pp. 56–69.

23 Runzo, 2008, p. 61.

24 See the helpful commentary on this by Peter W. Singer in his 'Frequently Asked Questions on the UCMJ Change and its Applicability to Private Military Contractors', 12 January 2007, www.pwsinger.com/commentary_070112.html (accessed 21 April 2009).

25 www.american.edu/sis/peacebuilding/security/traininginfo.htm (accessed 27 March 2007). At time of writing this particular training programme has ceased, but, according to the IPOA's Doug Brooks, similar programmes are likely to be run in conjunction with Human Rights Institutions in the near future (private email communication, 11 November 2009).

26 Runzo, 2008, p. 62.

27 Herfried Münkler, 2005, *The New Wars*, Cambridge: Polity Press, p. 134.

28 Robinson, 2007, p. 261.

29 Michael Walzer, 2008, 'Mercenary Impulse: Is there an ethics that justifies Blackwater?', *The New Republic*, 12 March, www.tnr.com/story.html?id=a498d530-e959-4f1e-8432-8851075ac657.

30 Peter D. Feaver, 2003, *Armed Servants: Agency, Oversight, and Civil–Military Relations*, Cambridge, MA: Harvard University Press.

31 Quoted in Cook, 2004, p. 59.

32 Ibid., p. 66.

33 For a lengthy discussion of this topic, see Mateo Taussig-Rubbo 2009, 'Outsourcing Sacrifice: The Labor of Private Military Contractors', *Yale Journal of Law & Humanities*, **2**(1), pp. 103–66.

34 Messner, 2007.

35 Ernesto Londoño, Joshua Partlow and Karen DeYoung, 'Contractor Helicopter Downed in Iraq', *Washington Post*, 24 January 2007, www.washingtonpost.com/wp-dyn/content/article/2007/01/23/AR 2007012300400_2.html (accessed 30 July 2009).

36 Marybeth Laguna 'My Husband Was a Blackwater Hero', *Washington Post*, 30 November 2008, www.washingtonpost.com/wp-dyn/content/article/2008/11/28/AR2008112802283.html (accessed 30 July 2009).

37 Ibid.

38 Walzer writes of his unwillingness to 'join the "moral giants" who would rather do nothing at all than send mercenaries to Darfur' (Walzer, 2008).

Chapter 4

1 Max Weber, 'Politics as a vocation' in *From Max Weber: essays in sociology*, trans., ed. and intr. H. H. Gerth and C. Wright Mills (Oxford: Oxford University Press, 1946), p. 78.

2 Ibid.

3 Owens, 2008, pp. 980–1.

4 For a useful account of how Locke's version of the social contract gives rise to a normative basis for the use of force, see M. J. Cresswell, 'Legitimizing Force: A Lockean Account', *Armed Forces & Society*, **30**(4), Summer 2004, pp. 629–48.

5 Fabre, 2008, p. 972.

6 Augustine of Hippo, *The City of God*, quoted in Cook, 2004, p. 43.

7 Cook, 2004, p. 44, italics in original.

8 Ibid., p. 46, italics in original.

9 David Rodin, 2002, *War and Self-Defense*, Oxford: Clarendon Press, p. 127.

10 Ibid., p. 129.

11 Ibid., p. 141.

12 Ibid., p. 162.

13 Rodin claims that the only way to avoid the problem he raises is through the creation of a global state, and for war to become a form of law-enforcement, ibid., p. 163ff.

14 Ibid., p. 142.

15 Ibid., p. 142.

16 Ibid., p. 143.

17 Ibid., p. 149.

18 Ibid., p. 151. This claim is, of course, contestable – it is entirely feasible that a case can be made that one does not need to be a participant in any particular common life in order to have a general recognition that that particular common life has value for those who do participate in it. I am grateful to Deborah Roberts for this point.

19 Ibid., p. 155.

20 Charles Taylor, 1985, 'Atomism' in *Philosophy and the Human Sciences: Philosophical Papers 2*, Cambridge: Cambridge University Press, p. 188.

21 Ibid., pp. 190–1.

22 Ibid., pp. 205–6.

23 As David Rodin has helpfully pointed out (in a personal communication), a useful analogy here might be that if I have the right to defend my life from unjustified attack with lethal force, then I have the right to defend with lethal force the necessary conditions of my continued survival from wrongful attack, for example in preventing the theft of my last food.

24 Deane-Peter Baker, 2006, 'Defending the Common Life: National Defence after Rodin', *Journal of Applied Philosophy*, **23**(3), pp. 259–75.

25 Rodin, op. cit., p. 152.

26 G. E. M. Anscombe, 1939, 'The Justice of the Present War Examined', republished in Anscombe, G. E. M. *Ethics, Religion and Politics: Collected Philosophical Papers: Vol. III*, Oxford: Blackwell, 1981.

27 Rodin, op. cit., p. 103.

28 James Turner Johnson, 1999, *Morality and Contemporary Warfare*, New Haven and London: Yale University Press, p. 29.

29 Cook, 2004, p. 123.

30 See, for example, David J. Garren, 2003, 'David Rodin's War and Self-Defense', *Journal of Military Ethics*, **2**(3), pp. 245–51.

31 Jeff McMahan, 2004, 'War as Self-Defense', *Ethics and International Affairs*, **18**(1), p. 80.

32 Fabre, op. cit.

33 It's worth noting, as Philip Bobbitt has pointed out, that this is an issue that doesn't only apply to private military companies and their employees: 'The United States has already found itself, in the Gulf War, in the position of providing intelligence and information to other states and selling its services as a war-making state.' (Philip Bobbitt, 2002, *The Shield of Achilles: War, Peace and the Course of History*, New York: Alfred A. Knopf, p. 305.)

34 Cook articulates Walzer's view well when he writes: 'Michael Walzer, in his fine book *Just and Unjust Wars*, attempts to work out why national loyalties should matter to people. His argument is that even though existing states and their boundaries result from arbitrary mapmaking and histories of conquest, reasonably good states can emerge, and the twin rights of territorial integrity and political sovereignty can create a "space" (both literal and metaphorical) where a group of people can attempt to work out a "common life".' (Cook, 2004, p. 49).

35 Walzer, 2008.

36 Charles Taylor, 1985, 'Atomism' in *Philosophy and the Human Sciences: Philosophical Papers 2* (Cambridge: Cambridge University Press), p. 188.

37 Owens, 2008, p. 982.

38 Ibid., p. 988.

39 Jurgen Brauer, 1999, 'An Economic Perspective on Mercenaries, Military Companies, and the Privatization of Force', *Cambridge Review of International Affairs*, **13**, Autumn/Winter, 1999, p. 2.

40 Owens, op. cit., p. 986.

41 Ibid, p. 988, the quote is from Peter W. Singer 2003, *Corporate Warriors: The Rise of the Privatized Military Industry*, Ithaca, NY: Cornell University Press, p. 217.

Chapter 5

1　Feaver, 2003, p. 65.

2　Pattison, 2008, p. 153.

3　Owens, 2008, pp. 986–7.

4　Krahmann, 2008, p. 258.

5　Christopher Spearin, 'Private Security Companies and Humanitarians: A Corporate Solution to Securing Humanitarian Spaces?', *International Peacekeeping*, **8**(1), Spring, 2001, p. 33.

6　Singer, 2003, p. 196.

7　Abdel-Fatau Musah and J. Kayode Fayemi, 2000, *Mercenaries: An African Security Dilemma*, London: Pluto Press, p. 27.

8　Samuel P. Huntington, 1957, *The Soldier and the State: The Theory and Politics of Civil–Military Relations*, Cambridge, MA: Harvard University Press, pp. 83–5 and passim.

9　Samuel P. Huntington, 1995, 'Reforming Civil–Military Relations', *Journal of Democracy*, **6**(4), pp. 9–10.

10　Huntington, 1957, pp. 83–5.

11　See for example John Allen Williams, 1995, 'The International Image of the Military Professional', *African Security Review*, **4**(5), pp. 24–7.

12　Feaver, 2003, p. 2.

13　As Feaver points out (Feaver 2003, p. 300), there is some evidence that the general presumption that the military is more likely to be correct than civilians on questions of national security is not necessarily accurate. In this Feaver points particularly to Eliot A. Cohen's important work *Supreme Command: Soldiers, Statesmen, and Leadership in Wartime* (New York: The Free Press, 2002).

14　Stephen Biddle and Stephen Long, 2004, 'Democracy and Military Effectiveness', *Journal of Conflict Resolution*, **48**(4), pp. 535–46.

15　Feaver, op. cit., p. 12.

16　Ibid., p. 55.

17　Cook, 2004, p. 74.

18　Feaver, op. cit., p. 3.

19　Cook, op. cit., p. 76.

20　Feaver, op. cit., p. 56.

21　Ibid., pp. 71–2.

22　Ibid., p. 72.

23 Huntington, 1957, p. 74.

24 Richard Kohn, 1997, 'How democracies control the military', *Journal of Democracy*, **8**(4), p. 143.

25 Feaver, op. cit., p. 89.

26 Ibid., p. 90.

27 Ibid., p. 234.

28 Ibid., p. 10.

29 Ibid., p. 90.

30 Ibid., p. 293.

31 Patrick J. McGowan, 2006, 'Coups and Conflict in West Africa, 1955–2004: Part II, Empirical Findings', *Armed Forces and Society*, **32**(2), p. 238.

32 Samuel Decalo, 1976, *Coups and Army Rule in Africa: Studies in Military Style*. New Haven, CT: Yale University Press, quoted in ibid., p. 238.

33 Ibid., pp. 248–9.

34 'The New Partnership for Africa's Development: The African Peer Review Mechanism', NEPAD Document, accessed at www.dfa.gov.za/au.nepad/nepad49.pdf on 4 December 2009.

35 McGowan, op. cit., p. 242.

36 Feaver, op. cit., p. 89.

Chapter 6

1 Feaver, 2003, p. 72.

2 Ibid., p. 54.

3 Krahmann, 2008, p. 255.

4 Münkler, 2005, pp. 134–5.

5 Pattison, 2008, p. 149.

6 Ibid., p. 151.

7 Feaver, op. cit., p. 57, italics added.

8 Singer, 2003, p. 226.

9 Feaver, op. cit., p. 55.

10 Deborah D. Avant, 2005, *The Market for Force: The Consequences of Privatizing Security*, Cambridge: Cambridge University Press, p. 43.

11 Feaver, 2003, p. 57.

12 Feaver, op. cit., p. 58.

13 P. W. Singer, 2003, 'Peacekeepers, Inc.' *Policy Review*, **119**, pp. 5–6. Available online at www.hoover.org/publications/policy-review/3448831.html (accessed 13 November 2008).

14 Feaver, 2003, p. 314, note 6. In the same footnote Feaver notes that in traditional civil–military relations 'the government enjoys a monopsony in purchasing security'. It is generally held that, in terms of social contract theory, it is essential that the state hold the monopoly on violence. This is a point that is sometimes raised to argue for the illegitimacy of private military companies. It's a nice question, however, whether it is not more accurate to say that social contract theory requires the state to have a *monopsony* with regard to violence. Unfortunately the constraints of this book do not allow me to pursue this question, though it is my hunch that this is indeed what is, in fact, implied by social contract theory. The undermining of this monopsony seems to me far more of a threat to appropriate civil–military relations than is the loss of the state military's monopoly on force.

15 Ibid., p. 60.

16 Ibid., p. 62.

17 Ibid., p. 62.

18 Ibid., p. 62.

19 Musah and Fayemi, 2000, p. 28.

20 Pattison, 2008, p. 153.

21 Feaver, op. cit., pp. 71–2.

22 Ibid., p. 73.

23 See for example the account of the complexities of battle-motivation in Chapter 7 of Richard Holmes' classic work, *Firing Line* (1985, Jonathon Cape: London).

24 Kohn, 1997, p. 143.

25 Thomas C. Bruneau and Florina Cristiana Matei, 2008, 'Towards a New Conceptualization of Democratization and Civil–Military Relations', *Democratization*, **15**(5), p. 922.

26 Feaver, op. cit., p. 69.

27 Ibid., p. 69.

28 Christopher Kinsey, 2008, 'Private security companies and corporate social responsibility' in Andrew Alexandra, Deane-Peter Baker and Marina Caparini (eds), *Private Military and Security Companies: Ethics,*

Policies and Civil–Military Relations, New York: Routledge, 2008), pp. 70–86.

29 Avant, 2005, p. 220.
30 Feaver, op. cit., pp. 72–3.
31 Ibid., p. 73.
32 Ibid., p. 74.
33 Singer, 2003, p. 222.
34 Feaver, op. cit., p. 74.

Chapter 7

1 Feaver, 2003, p. 75.
2 Singer, 2003, p. 220.
3 Hutchful, 2000, p. 222.
4 Singer, op. cit., pp. 214–15.
5 Feaver, op. cit., p. 85.
6 Avant, 2005, p. 220.
7 Christopher Spearin, 'Regulation and Control of Private Military Companies: The Legislative Dimension', *Contemporary Security Policy*, **26**(1), April 2005, p. 99.
8 Feaver, op. cit., p. 76.
9 Ibid., p. 77.
10 The idea of 'commander's intent' is designed to ensure unity of effort, while at the same time allowing subordinates the flexibility to make the tactical decisions that they believe to be most appropriate to the specific circumstances in which they find themselves engaged. It is a long-standing truism that no plan survives first contact, and successful military forces are usually those that have subordinate commanders with both the initiative and leeway to adapt quickly to a fast-changing environment. What unifies the efforts of these subordinate commanders is their understanding of the commanders' intent, that is the 'big picture' of what the overall commander seeks to achieve through the military operations in which they are engaged. (See J. L. Silva, 'Auftragstaktik', *Infantry*, September–October 1989, pp. 6–9.)
11 Thomas Ricks, 2009, *The Gamble: General David Petraeus and the*

American Military Adventure in Iraq, 2006–2008, Penguin Press, p. 269.

12 Ibid., p. 270.

13 In some developing world countries, state militaries do in fact directly involve themselves in economic ventures, often with the acquiescence of the civilian government. Where this happens, however, the effect is to reduce rather than enhance civilian control. See Herbert M. Howe, 2001, *Ambiguous Order: Military Forces in African States*, Boulder, CO: Lynne Rienner.

14 Feaver, op. cit., pp. 77–8.

15 Ibid., p. 78.

16 Avant, op. cit., pp. 68–9.

17 Feaver, op. cit., p. 78.

18 Ibid., p. 79.

19 Ibid., p. 79.

20 See for example the account in Howe, 2001.

21 Scahill, 2007, pp. 221–2.

22 Avant, op. cit., p. 61.

23 Christopher Spearin, 2005, 'Regulation and Control of Private Military Companies: The Legislative Dimension', *Contemporary Security Policy*, **26**, p. 99.

24 Jonathan Brown and Terri Judd, 'ArmorGroup sacks murder suspect', *The Independent*, 16 September 2009, www.independent.co.uk/news/world/middle-east/ArmorGroup-sacks-murder-suspect-17879 53.html (accessed 21 September 2009).

25 Feaver, op. cit., p. 80.

26 Ibid., p. 82.

27 Feaver points out that inter-service rivalry can also be thought of as an 'institutional check': 'Institutional checks are related to fire alarms, but the principal–agent literature usually treats them as distinct. An institutional check is a separate agent, established by the principal and empowered with a veto to block action of the other agent. The function of a simple fire alarm is to alert the principal, who will then intervene to punish or adjust behavior as needed. The function of an institutional check is more assertive – to block, either legally or in some cases physically, any behavior that might be considered untoward.' (p. 81.)

28 Feaver, 2003, p. 84.

29 Ibid., p. 84.

30 'Rice Issues New Rules for Blackwater', *Associated Press*, 8 October 2007, www.military.com/NewsContent/0,13319,151878,00.html? ESRC=eb.nl (accessed 12 October 2007).

31 Cook, 2004, p. 70.

32 Jody Ray Bennett, 4 May 2009, 'Triple Canopy, Obama's Blackwater', www.privateforces.com/index.php?option=com_content&task=vie w&id=2219&Itemid=1

33 Feaver, 2003, p. 89.

34 Herbert Wulf, 2008, 'Privatization of security, international interventions and the democratic control of armed forces' in Andrew Alexandra, Deane-Peter Baker, and Marina Caparini (eds) *Private Military and Security Companies: Ethics, Policies and Civil–Military Relations*, New York: Routledge, 2008), p. 194.

35 Pattison, 2008, p. 152.

36 Nathan Hodge, 'US seeks tighter control of war zone contractors', *Jane's Defense Weekly*, 15 August 2007, p. 15.

37 Feaver, 2003, p. 93.

38 Ibid., p. 95.

39 Isenberg, 2009, p. 15.

Chapter 8

1 Ignatieff, 1997, pp. 4–5.

2 Musah and Fayemi, 2000, p. 263.

3 See for example Mike Denning, 2004, 'A Prayer for Marie: Creating an Effective African Standby Force', *Parameters*, **34**(4), pp. 102–17.

4 United Nations Department of Peacekeeping Operations (DPKO), 2008 'Darfur – UNAMID – Background', available at <www.un.org/ Depts/dpko/missions/unamid/background.html> (accessed 12 August 09).

5 International Crisis Group (2008b) 'Conflict History: DR Congo', available at www.crisisgroup.org/home/index.cfm?action= conflict_search&l=1&t=1&c_country=37 (accessed 12 August 09).

6   Charter of the United Nations, accessed at www.un.org/en/
    documents/charter/chapter1.shtml (accessed 26 August 2009).

7   International Commission on Intervention and State Sovereignty
    (2001) *The Responsibility to Protect* (Ottowa: International Devel-
    opment Research Centre), p. xi.

8   For an account of why we might think that military humanitarian
    intervention is obligatory under certain circumstances, see Jovan
    Davidovic, 'Are Humanitarian Military Interventions Obligatory?',
    Journal of Applied Philosophy, **25**(2), 2008, pp. 134–44.

9   K. Annan, 2005, *In larger freedom: towards development, security and
    human rights for all*, Report of the Secretary General to the 59th
    Session of the United Nations General Assembly, (http://daccessdds.
    un.org/doc/UNDOC/GEN/N05/270/78/PDF/N0527078.
    pdf?OpenElement), p. 35. Emphasis in original.

10 For another account of the ground-breaking nature (in terms of
    international law) of the NATO intervention in Kosovo, see Prins, G.
    (2002), *The Heart of War: On Power, Conflict and Obligation in the
    Twenty-First Century* (London: Routledge), Chapter 5. From a legal
    perspective, Fernando Tesón (Tesón, F. (1997) *Humanitarian
    Intervention: An Inquiry into Law and Morality*, 2nd edn (Transnational
    Publishers Inc., Irvington-on-Hudson, NY), pp. 173–4), argues that:
    'The human rights imperative underlies the concepts of state and
    government and the precepts that are designed to protect them,
    most prominently article 2(4). The rights of states recognized by
    international law are meaningful only on the assumption that those
    states minimally observe individual rights. The United Nations
    purpose of promoting and protecting human rights found in article
    1(3), and by reference in article 2(4) as a qualifying clause to the pro-
    hibition of war, has a necessary primacy over the respect for state
    sovereignty. Force used in defense of fundamental human rights is
    therefore not a use of force inconsistent with the purposes of the
    United Nations.'

11 James Pattison, 2010, *Humanitarian Intervention and the Respon-
    sibility to Protect: Who should intervene?*, Oxford: Oxford University
    Press.

12 Pattison, 2010, Chapter 7. (In writing this and the next chapter I had
    access only to the pre-production draft of the book, as the book was

only published after this manuscript went to press. I have therefore avoided direct quotes, and have referenced only chapter numbers rather than page numbers.)

13 Pattison, 2010, Chapter 1.

14 Ibid.

15 Ibid.

16 Ibid.

17 Ibid., Chapter 2.

18 Mark S. Stein, 2004, 'Unauthorized Humanitarian Intervention', *Social Philosophy and Policy*, **21**(1), p. 37, quoted in Pattison 2010, Chapter 2.

19 Ryan Goodman, 2006, 'Humanitarian Intervention and Pretexts for War', *American Journal of International Law*, **100**(1), p. 116, quoted in Pattison 2010, Chapter 2.

20 Walzer, 2008.

21 Alan Kuperman, 2001, *The Limits of Humanitarian Intervention: Genocide in Rwanda*, Washington DC: Brookings Institution Press, p. 116, quoted in Pattison 2010, Chapter 3.

22 Here Pattison is distinguishing between perceived legitimacy and actual legitimacy. An intervention can, in theory, be legitimate without being widely perceived to be so, or it can be perceived to be legitimate but in fact not be. Perceived legitimacy is a factor in the effectiveness of the intervention, as it is likely to make it easier for the intervener to achieve its operational goals. (Pattison 2010, Chapter 3.)

23 Pattison recommends a number of interesting amendments to the traditional 'external' principles of *jus in bello*, which we need not go into for the purposes of this book, but can simply grant for the sake of argument. (Pattison 2010, Chapter 4.)

24 Pattison argues against the use of conscripts on the grounds that conscription is at odds with individual autonomy and freedom of conscience. (Pattison 2010, Chapter 4.)

25 I owe this point to Michael Pitchford, though I have modified it somewhat from his original articulation of the problem.

Chapter 9

1 Fabre, 2008, p. 969.

2 It is not, however, inconceivable. See, for example, Christopher M. Rochester, 2007. 'A Private Alternative to a Standing UN Peacekeeping Force', Peace Operations Institute White Paper, Washington, DC: Peace Operations Institute *(peaceops.org/poi/images/stories/poi_ wp_privatealternative.pdf* (accessed 7 October 2009). Interestingly, Tobias Masterton and others have put forward the idea of a non-profit private military company that works exclusively for the United Nations (See www.corpwatch.org/article.php?id=8989, accessed 7 October 2009).

3 Cancian, 2008, p. 65.

4 In 2009 the United Nations was facing a 35 per cent shortage of deployed police for its peacekeeping missions, compared with 'only' a 20 per cent shortage of deployed troops (Mark Turner, 2009, 'Doing the Work: An Overview of United Nations Missions' in Dulcie Leimbach (ed.), *A Global Agenda: Issues Before the United Nations 2009–2010*, New York: United Nations Association of the United States of America, p. 15).

5 www.royalnavy.mod.uk/operations-and-support/surface-fleet/ patrol-vessels/fishery-protection-squadron/offshore-patrol-vessel-helicopter/ (accessed 10 September 2009).

6 Hugh Smith, 'What Costs will Democracies Bear? A Review of Popular Theories of Casualty Aversion', *Armed Forces & Society*, **31**(4), Summer 2005, pp. 487–512.

7 Cancian, 2008, p. 72.

8 NATO information sheet. www.nato.int/issues/nrf/index.html (accessed 23 September 2009).

9 See, for example, Deane-Peter Baker and Sadiki Maeresera, 'SADCBRIG intervention in SADC member states: Reasons to doubt', *African Security Review* 2009, **18**(1), pp. 106–10.

10 Henri Boshoff, *ISS Today*, 16 October 2007: ISS Responds to attack on AMIS Peacekeepers, Part 2: The Haskanita Incident and the Challenges Facing the AU-UN Hybrid Force to Darfur. www.issafrica. org/index.php?link_id=29&slink_id=5076&link_type=12&slink_type =12&tmpl_id=3 (accessed 23 September 2009).

11   Quoted in Beckett, 2007, p. 79.

12   Cook, 2004, pp. 123–4.

13   For an account of the difficulty of legitimizing force at the international level see M. J. Cresswell, 'Legitimizing Force: A Lockean
Account', *Armed Forces & Society*, **30**(4), Summer 2004, p. 639. Cecile
Fabre, by contrast, contends strongly for a cosmopolitan account of
the use of armed force that would legitimate any body able to
protect human rights. (Fabre 2008, pp. 968–71.)

14   Olsthoorn, 2005, p. 184.

15   Gross, 2008, pp. 214–15.

16   Ibid., p. 218.

17   It is comforting to know that I am in good company in holding this
intuition:

   'Is there the same duty to risk one's life and die for humanity that
   there is, generally, to risk one's life for the state? Many people
   think there is not. Commenting on the United State's ill-fated
   mission to stabilize Somalia in 1993, Samuel Huntington was
   unequivocal. "It is morally unjustifiable and politically indefensi-
   ble," he writes, "that members of the Armed Forces should be
   killed to prevent Somalis from killing one another . . . The military
   should only be given military missions which involve possible
   combat when they advance national security interests which are
   directed against a foreign enemy of the United States."' (Ibid.,
   p. 213).

18   Ibid.

19   Owens, 2008, pp. 978–9. The quote is from Avant, p. 26.

Conclusion

1   Nicholas Rennger and Caroline Kennedy-Pipe, 2008, 'The State of
War', *International Affairs* **84**(5), p. 901.

2   Philip Bobbitt, 2002, *The Shield of Achilles: War, Peace and the Course
of History*, New York: Alfred A. Knopf.

3   Philip Bobbitt, 2008, *Terror and Consent: The Wars for the Twenty-First
Century*, London: Allen Lane.

4   Bobbitt is also Distinguished Senior Lecturer at the University of

Texas Law School and Senior Fellow in the Robert S. Strauss Center for International Security and Law at the University of Texas.

5 Not to be confused with the 'war on terror', which is also sometimes referred to as the 'long war'.

6 Bobbitt, 2002, p. 211.

7 Ibid., p. 304.

8 Ibid., p. 242.

9 Cook, 2004, p. 59.

10 See for example James O'Connell, 'The Development of a Paralegal Profession in the United Kingdom', *Journal of Commonwealth Law and Legal Education*, 1750-662X, **5**(2), 1 October 2007, pp. 97–109.

11 David Isenberg, 2009, 'Private Military Contractors and U.S. Grand Strategy', PRIO Report 1/2009, International Peace Research Institute, Oslo (PRIO), www.prio.no/sptrans/-1720057691/Isenberg%20 Private%20Military%20Contractors%20PRIO%20Report%201-2009. pdf (accessed 21/10/2009), p. 12.

12 Jürgen Brauer, 1999, 'An economic perspective on mercenaries, military companies, and the privatisation of force', *Cambridge Review of International Affairs*, **13**(1), p. 135.

13 Bobbitt, op. cit., p. 277.

14 French, 2003, p. 10.

15 Isenberg, 2009, p. 44.

16 'An analogy can be made to the use of reserve units. For most of the twentieth century reservists were regarded as second-string players who would be useful only in an emergency. The active-duty force was much easier to train, employ, and control. Gradually, however, driven by necessity, planners learned how to integrate reserve forces to the point where such actions are now routine. The same evolution should take place for contractors. The issue is not whether we need them – we do – the real issue is how rapidly can we build the structures, doctrine, and strategy to employ them effectively.' (Cancian 2008, p. 76.)

17 Fabre, op. cit., p. 970.

18 Ibid., p. 971.

Bibliography

Scott Anderson (2002), 'Prostitution and sexual autonomy: Making sense of the prohibition of prostitution', in *Ethics* 112 (4), pp. 748–80.

G. E. M. Anscombe (1939), 'The Justice of the Present War Examined', republished in Anscombe, G. E. M. (1981), *Ethics, Religion and Politics: Collected Philosophical Papers vol. III*, Oxford: Blackwell.

Deborah D. Avant (2005), *The Market for Force: The Consequences of Privatizing Security*. Cambridge: Cambridge University Press.

Deane-Peter Baker (2006), 'Defending the Common Life: National Defence after Rodin', in *Journal of Applied Philosophy*, 23 (3), pp. 259–75.

Deane-Peter Baker and Sadiki Maeresera (2009), 'SADCBRIG intervention in SADC member states: Reasons to doubt', in *African Security Review*, 18 (1), pp. 106–10.

Eeben Barlow (2007), *Executive Outcomes: Against all Odds*, Johannesburg: Galago Press.

Stephen Biddle and Stephen Long (2004), 'Democracy and Military Effectiveness', in *Journal of Conflict Resolution*, 48 (4), pp. 535–46.

Philip Bobbitt, (2002), *The Shield of Achilles: War, Peace and the Course of History*, New York, NY: Alfred A. Knopf.

Philip Bobbitt (2008), *Terror and Consent: The Wars for the Twenty-First Century*, London: Allen Lane.

Mark Bowden (1999), *Black Hawk Down: A Story of Modern War*. Berkeley, CA: Atlantic Monthly Press.

Jürgen Brauer (1999), 'An economic perspective on mercenaries, military companies, and the privatisation of force', in *Cambridge Review of International Affairs*, Volume 13, Issue 1, 1999, pp. 130–46.

Doug Brooks and Matan Chorev (2008), 'Ruthless humanitarianism: why marginalizing private peacekeeping kills people', in Andrew Alexandra, Deane-Peter Baker and Marina Caparini (eds), *Private Military and Security Companies: Ethics, policies and civil-military relations*, London and New York, NY: Routledge, pp. 116–30.

Thomas C. Bruneau and Florina Cristiana Matei (2008), 'Towards a New Conceptualization of Democratization and Civil–Military Relations', in *Democratization*, 15 (5), pp. 909–29.

Mark Cancian (2008), 'Contractors: The New Element of Military Force Structure', *Parameters*, Autumn, pp. 61–77.

C. A. J. Coady (1992), 'Mercenary Morality', in *International Law and Armed Conflict*, A. G. D. Bradney (ed.), Stuttgart: Steiner, pp 55–69.

Anthony Coates (2006), 'Culture, the Enemy and the Moral Restraint of War', in *The Ethics of War: Shared Problems in Different Traditions,* Richard Sorabji and David Rodin (eds) (2006), Aldershot: Ashgate, pp. 208–21.

Eliot A. Cohen (2002), *Supreme Command: Soldiers, Statesmen, and Leadership in Wartime*, New York: The Free Press.

Christopher Coker (2004), *The Future of War*, London: Wiley Blackwell.

Martin Cook (2004), *The Moral Warrior: Ethics and Service in the U.S. Military*, New York, NY: State University of New York Press.

M. J. Cresswell (2004), 'Legitimizing Force: A Lockean Account' *Armed Forces & Society*, Vol. 30, No. 4, 629–48

Jovan Davidovic (2008), 'Are Humanitarian Military Interventions Obligatory?', in *Journal of Applied Philosophy*, Vol. 25, No. 2, pp. 134–44

Samuel Decalo (1976), *Coups and Army Rule in Africa: Studies in Military Style*, New Haven, CT: Yale University Press.

Mike Denning (2004), 'A Prayer for Marie: Creating an Effective African Standby Force', in *Parameters,* 34 (4), pp. 102–17.

Lars Ericsson (1980), 'Charges against Prostitution: An Attempt at a Philosophical Assessment', *Ethics* 90 (3) pp. 335–66

Cécile Fabre (2010) 'In Defence of Mercenarism', in *British Journal of Political Science*, forthcoming.

Peter D. Feaver (2003), *Armed Servants: Agency, Oversight, and Civil-Military Relations*. Cambridge, MA: Harvard University Press.

Shannon E. French (2003), *The Code of the Warrior: Exploring Warrior Values Past and Present*, New York, NY: Rowman and Littlefield.

Mervyn Frost (2008), 'Regulating anarchy: The ethics of PMCs in global civil society', in Andrew Alexandra, Deane-Peter Baker and Marina Caparini (eds), *Private Military and Security Companies: Ethics, policies and civil-military relations*, London and New York, NY: Routledge, pp. 43–55.

David J. Garren, (2003), 'David Rodin's War and Self-Defense', in *Journal of Military Ethics*, 2 (3), pp. 245–51

Ryan Goodman (2006), 'Humanitarian Intervention and Pretexts for War', in *American Journal of International Law*, 100 (1), pp. 107–41

Michael L. Gross, (2008). 'Is there a Duty to die for Humanity? Humanitarian Intervention, Military Service and Political Obligation', in *Public Affairs Quarterly*, 22 (3), pp. 213–29.

David Grossman (2004), *On Combat: The psychology and physiology of deadly conflict in war and peace*, PPCT Research Publications.

Sabelo Gumedze (2007) 'Towards the revision of the *1977 OAU/AU Convention on the Elimination of Mercenarism in Africa*', *African Security Review* 16 (4), pp. 22–33.

Richard Holmes (1985), *Firing Line*, London: J. Cape.

Herbert M. Howe (2001), *Ambiguous Order: Military Forces in African States*, Boulder CO: Lynne Rienner.

Samuel P. Huntington (1957), *The Soldier and the State: The Theory and Politics of Civil–Military Relations*, Cambridge, MA: Harvard University Press.

Samuel P. Huntington (1995), 'Reforming Civil-Military Relations', in *Journal of Democracy*, 6(4), pp. 9–10.

Michael Ignatieff (1997), *The Warrior's Honor: Ethnic War and the Modern Conscience*, New York: Metropolitan Books.

International Commission on Intervention and State Sovereignty (2001), *The Responsibility to Protect*, Ottawa: International Development Research Centre.

James Turner Johnson (1999), *Morality and Contemporary Warfare*, New Haven and London: Yale University Press.

Asa Kasher (2008), 'Interface Ethics: Military Forces and Private Military Companies', in Andrew Alexandra, Deane-Peter Baker and Marina Caparini (eds), *Private Military and Security Companies: Ethics, Policies and Civil–Military Relations,* New York: Routledge, pp. 235–46.

Christopher Kinsey (2008), 'Private security companies and corporate social responsibility', in Andrew Alexandra, Deane-Peter Baker and Marina Caparini (eds), *Private Military and Security Companies: Ethics, Policies and Civil-Military Relations*, New York: Routledge, pp. 70–86.

Richard Kohn (1997), 'How democracies control the military', in *Journal of Democracy*, 8 (4) pp. 140–53.

Elke Krahmann (2008), 'The new model soldier and civil–military relations', in Andrew Alexandra, Deane-Peter Baker and Marina Caparini (eds), *Private Military and Security Companies: Ethics, Policies and Civil-Military Relations*, New York: Routledge, pp. 247–65.

Alan Kuperman (2001), *The Limits of Humanitarian Intervention: Genocide in Rwanda*, Washington DC: Brookings Institution Press.

Marcus Luttrell (2007), *Lone Survivor: The Eyewitness Account of Operation Redwing and the Lost Heroes of Seal Team 10*, New York: Little Brown and Company.

Heidi L. Maibom and Fred Bennett (2009), 'Patriotic Virtue', in *Political Studies*, 57 (3), pp. 639–59.

Robert MacCoun, Kier, E. and Belkin, A. (2006). 'Does social cohesion determine motivation in combat? An old question with an old answer', in *Armed Forces and Society*, 32 (2), pp. 646–54.

Patrick J. McGowan (2003), 'African military coups d'état, 1956–2001: frequency, trends and distribution', in *Journal of Modern African Studies* (2003), 41 (3), pp. 339–70.

Patrick J. McGowan (2006), 'Coups and Conflict in West Africa, 1955-2004: Part II, Empirical Findings', in *Armed Forces and Society*, 32 (2), pp. 234–53.

Jeff McMahan (2004), 'War as Self-Defense', in *Ethics and International Affairs*, 18 (1), pp. 75–80.

William Ian Miller (2000), *The Mystery of Courage*, Cambridge, MA; Harvard University Press.

Thomas More (1974), *Utopia: A Dialogue of Comfort*, London: Heron Books.

Charles Moskos Jr. (1986), 'Institutional/Occupational Trends in Armed Forces: An Update', in *Armed Forces & Society*, 12 (3). pp. 377–82.

Herfried Münkler (2005), *The New Wars*, Cambridge: Polity Press

Abdel-Fatau Musah and J. 'Kayode Fayemi (eds) (2000), *Mercenaries: An African Security Dilemma*, London: Pluto Press

James O'Connell (2007), 'The Development of a Paralegal Profession in the United Kingdom', *Journal of Commonwealth Law and Legal Education*, 5 (2), 97–109

Peter Olsthoorn (2005), 'Honor as a Motive for Making Sacrifices', in *Journal of Military Ethics*, 4 (3), pp. 183–97.

Peter Olsthoorn (2007), 'Courage in the Military: Physical and Moral' in *Journal of Military Ethics* 6 (4), pp. 270–9.

Mark Osiel (2001), *Obeying Orders: Atrocity, Military Discipline, and the Law of War*, Piscataway, NJ: Transaction Publishers.

Patricia Owens, (2008), 'Distinctions, distinctions: 'public' and 'private' force?', in *International Affairs*, 84: 5 (2008), pp. 977–90.

Carole Pateman (1983), 'Defending Prostitution: Charges Against Ericcson', in *Ethics* 93 (3), pp. 561–5.

James Pattison (2008), 'Just War Theory and the Privatization of Military Force', *Ethics & International Affairs*, 22 (2), pp. 143–62.

James Pattison (2010), *Humanitarian Intervention and the Responsibility to Protect: Who should intervene?*, Oxford: Oxford University Press.

Sarah Percy (2007), *Mercenaries: the history of a norm in International Relations*, Oxford: Oxford University Press.

J. G. Peristiany (ed.) (1968), *Honour and Shame: The Values of Mediterranean Society*, London: Weidenfeld and Nicolson.

Gwyn Prins (2002), *The Heart of War: On Power, Conflict and Obligation in the Twenty-First Century* London: Routledge.

Nicholas Rengger and Caroline Kennedy-Pipe (2008), 'The State of War', *International Affairs* 84 (5), pp. 891–902.

Thomas Ricks (2009), *The Gamble: General David Petraeus and the American Military Adventure in Iraq, 2006–2008*, Penguin Press.

Paul Robinson 2007, 'Magnanimity and Integrity as Military Virtues', in *Journal of Military Ethics* 6 (4), pp. 259–69.

Christopher M. Rochester (2007), 'A Private Alternative to a Standing UN Peacekeeping Force', in Peace Operations Institute White Paper, Washington, DC: Peace Operations Institute.

David Rodin (2002), *War and Self-Defense*, Oxford: Clarendon Press.

Joseph Runzo (2008), 'Benevolence, honourable soldiers and private military companies: Reformulating Just War theory', in Andrew Alexandra, Deane-Peter Baker and Marina Caparini (eds), *Private Military and Security Companies: Ethics, Policies and Civil–Military Relations*, New York: Routledge, pp. 56–69.

Jeremy Scahill (2007), *Blackwater: The Rise of the World's Most Powerful Mercenary Army* (1st edn) New York, NY: Nation Books.

Peter W. Singer (2003), *Corporate Warriors: The Rise of the Privatized Military Industry*, Ithaca, NY: Cornell University Press.

Peter W. Singer (2003), 'Peacekeepers, Inc.', in *Policy Review*, 119, pp. 5–6

Quentin Skinner (1978), *The Foundations of Modern Political Thought: Vol. 1, The Rennaissance*, Cambridge: Cambridge University Press.

Hugh Smith (2005), 'What Costs will Democracies Bear? A Review of Popular Theories of Casualty Aversion', in *Armed Forces & Society*, 31 (4), pp. 487–512

Christopher Spearin (2001), 'Private Security Companies and Humanitarians: A Corporate Solution to Securing Humanitarian Spaces?', in *International Peacekeeping* 8 (1), pp. 20–43.

Christopher Spearin (2005), 'Regulation and Control of Private Military Companies: The Legislative Dimension', in *Contemporary Security Policy*, 26 (1), pp. 84–102.

Mark S. Stein (2004), 'Unauthorized Humanitarian Intervention', in *Social Philosophy and Policy*, 21 (1), pp. 14–38.

Uwe Steinhoff (2008), 'What are mercenaries?', in Andrew Alexandra, Deane-Peter Baker and Marina Caparini (eds), *Private Military and Security Companies: Ethics, Policies and Civil–Military Relations*, New York: Routledge, pp. 19–20.

Mateo Taussig-Rubbo (2009), 'Outsourcing Sacrifice: The Labor of Private Military Contractors', in *Yale Journal of Law & Humanities*, 2 (1), pp. 103–66.

Charles Taylor (1985), *Philosophy and the Human Sciences: Philosophical Papers 2*, Cambridge: Cambridge University Press.

Fernando Tesón (1997), *Humanitarian Intervention: An Inquiry into Law and Morality*, 2nd edn, Irvington-on-Hudson, NY: Transnational Publishers Inc.

James Toner (1995), *True Faith and Allegiance: The Burden of Military Ethics*, Lexington, KY: University of Kentucky Press.

Mark Turner (2009), 'Doing the Work: An Overview of United Nations Missions', in Dulcie Leimbach (ed.), *A Global Agenda: Issues Before the United Nations 2009–2010*, New York: United Nations Association of the United States of America.

Adrian Walsh and Tony Lynch (2000), 'The Good Mercenary?', in *Journal of Political Philosophy*, 8 (2), 133–53.

Max Weber (1946), 'Politics as a vocation', in *From Max Weber: essays in sociology*, trans., ed. and intr. H. H. Gerth and C. Wright Mills, New York: Oxford University Press, pp. 77–128.

John Allen Williams (1995), 'The International Image of the Military Professional', in *African Security Review* 4(5), 24–7

Herbert Wulf (2008), 'Privatization of security, international interventions and the democratic control of armed forces', in Andrew Alexandra, Deane-Peter Baker and Marina Caparini (eds), *Private Military and Security Companies: Ethics, Policies and Civil–Military Relations*, New York: Routledge, pp. 191–202.

Index